TREES OF THE
ROCKY MOUNTAINS
AND INTERMOUNTAIN WEST

A new and simple way to identify and
enjoy all the trees that grow wild in

INTERIOR ALASKA, YUKON,

E. BRITISH COLUMBIA, SW. ALBERTA,

E. WASHINGTON, E. OREG___

IDAH_ _____ __H,

WN
BRARY

by
GEORGE A. PETRIDES

**Illustrated by
OLIVIA PETRIDES**

BACKPACKER FIELD GUIDE SERIES ®

582.16
P44R
2000

BACKPACKER FIELD GUIDE SERIES [®]
Published by Explorer Press[™]
P.O. Box 233, Williamston, Michigan 48895

Copyright ©2000 by George A. Petrides and Olivia Petrides

Manufactured in the United States of America

ISBN 0-9646674-2-8

Library of Congress Catalogue Card Number: 97-61669

Petrides, George A. and Olivia Petrides
Bibliography: pp. 99-100
Index, pp. 101-107

1. Tree Identification - Handbooks, Manuals, etc.
2. Forestry - Silviculture.
3. Arboretums - Natural Areas.
4. Natural Areas - Rocky Mountains and Intermountain Region
5. National Parks - Rocky Mountains and Intermountain Region
6. National Forests - Rocky Mountains and Intermountain Region
7. Vegetation - Trees of the Rocky Mountains, Great Basin, etc.
8. Ecology - Trees, Rocky Mountains /Intermountain Region
9. Canada - Trees of the Rocky Mountains
10. Alaska - Trees of the Rocky Mountains/Interior Alaska

Base map from Little (1971)
Cover photo: Wyoming Rocky Mountains

CONTENTS

The Rocky Mountain and Intermountain Regions

The Rocky Mountains comprise a discontinuous series of ranges that extend from Alaska to Mexico and beyond. For thousands of miles, the main range forms the Continental Divide from whose meandering crest rainwaters drain both eastward to streams like the Mackenzie, Missouri, and Rio Grande and westward into the Fraser, Columbia, Colorado, and other rivers.

Some of the world's finest forests blanket the slopes and valleys of these western mountains. In national parks and other scenic sites of both the United States and Canada, geysers, hot springs, glaciers, and other natural attractions add further interest to these remarkable landscapes. Visitors from around the world are thrilled by the magnificent timberlands, lakes, streams, waterfalls, peaks, and wildlife that grace these mountain chains.

Between the Rockies and the major mountains of coastal states and provinces, other forests and woodlands occur. The Great Basin, in particular, is a vast arid region that has no drainage outlet to the sea. Yet this intermountain region, centered on Nevada, contains many isolated mountain ranges whose higher slopes are mostly forested.

Geographic Scope of this Book

The tree flora of the nine entire states and provinces listed on the title page as well as portions of six additional such units is described in this book. Though coastal and inland trees of the Pacific Coast states and provinces are both described in our *Trees of the Pacific Northwest*, the inland species contribute also to forests of the Rocky Mountain and intermountain regions. They are reviewed here again. On the eastern slopes of the Rockies, the limits of tree growth are usually evident in the field. Southward, for our purposes, West Texas is bounded to the east by projecting the eastern border of New Mexico south to the Rio Grande.

Like the Mexican birds of the international boundary region, the Mexican trees that extend their ranges northward into the southwestern United States are of great interest to naturalists. Our forthcoming *Trees of the American Southwest* offers an enlarged text and more fully illustrates those species. Nevertheless, to ensure complete coverage of trees in the Rocky Mountain and Intermountain regions and to satisfy the immediate interests of readers, the principal field marks of all southwestern trees are included here.

A Note from the Author

I first became interested in the identification of trees and shrubs while studying the food preferences of deer during their critical winter season. It was important to identify not only the twigs browsed by deer but also those that the animals neglected or avoided as foods. Even though leaves were absent, these plants had to be identified quickly while snowshoeing along cruise lines through the forest. Ever since then, I have tried to detect or confirm field marks that would easily identify a woody plant at any season, not just when flowers, fruits, or even leaves were present.

Acknowledgements

I wish to thank Dr. William A. Weber of the University of Colorado Museum for his many helpful suggestions. Dr. Leslie R. Landrum of Arizona State University advised regarding trees of his state. Dr. Stephen N. Stevenson, Associate Professor of Botany at Michigan State University, and Dr. Ronald L. Hartman of the Department of Botany at the University of Wyoming, also reviewed the text and offered improvements. Thanks are due, too, to Dr. Gustaaf A. de Zoeten, Professor and Chairman of the Department of Botany, and Dr. Alan Prather, Curator, who graciously made available the fine collection of Rocky Mountains plants that forms a part of the Michigan State University herbarium.

My daughter, Olivia, Adjunct Associate Professor at the School of the Art Institute of Chicago, provided the clear art work for this book and others in this series. She also painted the nice color illustrations for our more comprehensive *Field Guide to Western Trees.* I wish to express my appreciation to her, sincerely, for her fine work, to Kristen Hadjoglou who assisted with the art work, and to Tom Greensfelder, graphic artist, who helped greatly toward improved computerization. — George A. Petrides

Disclaimer

This book mentions that certain fruits and plant parts may be eaten or used for medicinal purposes.Though gleaned from reputable sources this information, however, has not been verified. It is recommended that no plant parts be taken internally unless medical experts or other authoritative sources declare that it is safe to do so.

It is also noted that certain plants have been used in the past to disable fish—a practice now illegal and certainly unsportsmanlike. With present-day needs for ecological awareness, it is trusted that no one will attempt to misuse this practice of pioneer days.

This book is intended to help residents and visitors enjoy the magnificent forests and landscapes of the region by increasing their ability to identify the trees. The author and Explorer Press™ are not liable or responsible for any damage/injury/loss caused, or said to be caused, directly or indirectly by statements found in this volume.

HOW TO USE THIS BOOK

Please read this section! It will answer your most frequently-asked questions.

As with our *Field Guide to Western Trees* (Houghton Mifflin Co., 1992), this smaller book is designed for convenient field use. It provides guidelines that will identify any tree that grows wild in the Rockies and Intermountain West, and at any season not just when it is in leaf or in flower.

All 215 trees native to or naturalized in our region are considered. They are divided into 42 small groups comprised of species that look alike whether or not they are related. Within each group, similarities and differences are pointed out.

Botanical terms are avoided; simple language is used throughout. Nevertheless, scientific as well as common names are given so that, if desired, descriptions in other books can be compared accurately.

The book is divided into six sections (I-VI):

1.	Leaves needlelike or scalelike (conifers).	**I. Plates 1-10**
1.	Leaves broad:	
	2. Leaves opposite or whorled:	
	3. Leaves compound.	**II. Plates 11-12**
	3. Leaves simple.	**III. Plates 13-14**
	2. Leaves alternate:	
	4. Leaves compound.	**IV. Plate 15-20**
	4. Leaves simple.	**V. Plates 21-40**
1.	Yuccas, palms, cacti	**VI. Plates 41-42**

In choosing the proper section for broadleaf trees, it is essential that the **difference between simple and compound leaves** be understood (see below and Figure 1, page 8).

A **simple** leaf has only one broad *blade* with a central *midrib*. The basal portion of the midrib forms a *leafstalk* which is attached to the twig. The leafstalk is mostly not woody and can be detached readily from the *woody* twig. A **compound** leaf also has a midrib but to it are attached a number of *separate leaflets*.

When the leafstalk of either a simple or compound leaf separates from the twig, it leaves a *leaf scar* that contains tiny dots known as *bundle scars* (use lens). A *bud* also normally remains nearby. When a leaf*let* becomes detached from the midrib only an indefinite mark of attachment is evident and *no* bud is present. In contrast to **alternate** leaves, **opposite** leaves occur in pairs (note the positions of buds and leaf scars in Figure 2, page 9).

In this book, a **twig** is not just any small division of a branch. Rather it is only the end portion, the part that constitutes the newest growth.

A **branchlet** is the previous year's growth, separated from the twig by a series of encircling *end-bud scars* (Fig.1). The term branchlet also is used for any small branch that is not a twig.

This book follows the U.S. Forest Service definition of a **tree**: a woody plant at least 13 feet (4 m) tall with a single trunk at least three inches (7.5 cm.) in diameter at breast height. Trees not described as **evergreen** can be assumed to be **deciduous**.

Identifying Unknown Trees —

Collecting plants for identification and study is a practice that has long been sanctioned by science. Collections should be made, however, in moderation and under suitable conditions. Collecting wild plants must be balanced against the need to preserve natural values. In some areas, including national and state parks and monuments, it is *illegal* to collect plants without a permit.

From the standpoint of making an accurate identification, *it is better to make identifications in the field than to collect specimens to be named at home or in camp.* When collected specimens are examined later, you may find that important characteristics such as milky sap, spicy odors, bark pattern, and growth habits had not been noted. Fallen leaves and fruits that might have provided useful clues to identification also may have been overlooked.

If, nevertheless, you find it desirable to collect a specimen for later study, keep in mind that *a good specimen is essential for correct identification.* Avoid dwarfed, twisted, and gnarled branches. From a vigorous specimen, clip six inches to a foot of the branch tip so that both leaf and twig characteristics are present.

With the unknown tree or specimen at hand and turning to the proper section of the book, you can scan the several plates and select the species that most resembles the unknown plant. When leaves are absent, use the leafless key at the end of the book as well as the illustrations and text descriptions.

Equipment—

Fortunately, the field identification of trees requires a minimum of equipment. Only a field guide and a pocket hand lens are needed. *A good hand lens is as essential to the botanical naturalist as binoculars are to the birder.* A lens that magnifies 6x to 10x will not only disclose the beauty hidden in small blossoms but will be of great help in checking on the hairiness of leaves and twigs, the presence or absence of leafstalk glands, and other details. Holding the lens *near your eye* makes it almost part of you and usually enhances your field of vision.

FIG. I: LEAF AND TWIG TERMINOLOGY

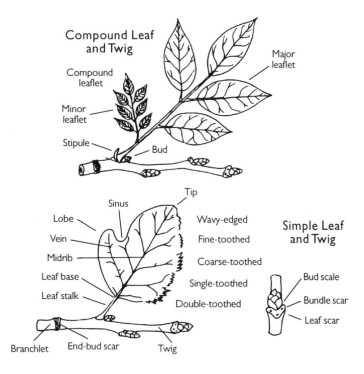

Compound Leaf and Twig

- Compound leaflet
- Minor leaflet
- Stipule
- Bud
- Major leaflet

- Tip
- Sinus
- Lobe
- Vein
- Midrib
- Leaf base
- Leaf stalk
- Wavy-edged
- Fine-toothed
- Coarse-toothed
- Single-toothed
- Double-toothed
- Branchlet
- End-bud scar
- Twig

Simple Leaf and Twig

- Bud scale
- Bundle scar
- Leaf scar

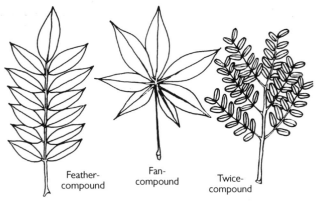

Feather-compound

Fan-compound

Twice-compound

Reprinted from *A Field Guide to Western Trees*, Houghton Mifflin Co., 1992

8

FIG. 2: TWIG AND BUD TERMINOLOGY

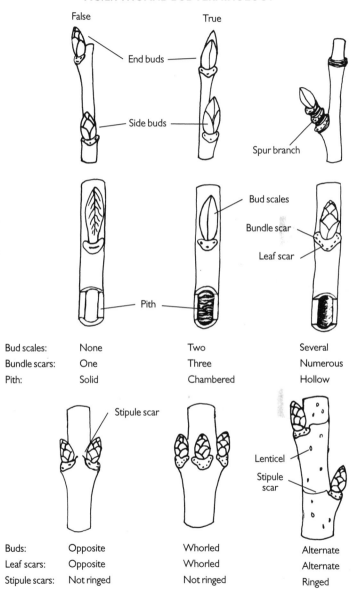

Reprinted from A Field Guide to Western Trees, Houghton Mifflin Co., 1992

Plant Names —

In this book, common names that include the name of another unrelated group, for example Douglas-fir or Redcedar, are either hyphenated or joined together to indicate that they are not true members of the group.

Although common names are well established for some species, often such names vary from one part of the country to another – and from one book to another. In consequence, scientific names are established to provide standardized designations for each species.

Scientific names have three essential parts: the name of the *genus* (plural *genera*), the name of the *species* (plural *species*), and the name or names, commonly abbreviated, of the botanist(s) who assigned the name and who stand(s) as the authority(ies) behind it. The generic name (but not the specific name) is capitalized.

Unfortunately, scientific names also may change as continued study indicates that a species is more closely related to members of a different group, that plants once thought to be two species should be combined as mere varieties of one species, that a species originally thought to be new has already been named, and so forth. Scientific names tend to be anglicized when spoken. One should not hesitate to use them. Anyone who can say *arbutus*, *rhododendron*, or *yucca* is already using scientific names. In speech, the authors' names are usually omitted.

The Flora of North America (Morin 1993, 1997), now in development, is becoming the basic reference for plant names and classification in the region. The scientific names accepted by specialists who compiled the first volumes of this continuing series are used in this book. For species not yet reached by that flora, two sources are utilized. For Rocky Mountain and Intermountain trees that also occur in California, the names of Hickman (1993) and his collaborators are adopted. For other species, the names listed are mostly those of Little (1979). Full citations of these references are given on pages 99-100. Unless markedly distinctive in the field (i.e. Arizona Pine, Lombardy Poplar), varieties or other subdivisions of species are not emphasized.

Measurements —

Measurements are given in English units of feet ('), inches ("), and fractions where appropriate in the text. See the ruler on page 109 for metric conversions of small measurements, or recall that 1" = 2.5 cm, 1' = 30.5 cm, 3.3' = 1 m.

Factors Affecting the Survival and Distribution of Trees —

The aggregation of trees that occurs in any locality is determined first by the parent trees present and then largely by the interacting factors of climate, soil, and other living things. Temperature and precipitation affect the survival of each tree species (especially that of seedlings) and also determine the characteristics of the soil upon which trees depend for much of their nutrient intake. Other species may cause competition, disease, parasitism, browsing, etc.

Differences in altitude cause climates, soils, and vegetation to vary greatly between locations. In mountainous terrain, tree floras only a fraction of a mile apart may be quite different from each other — and, in consequence, support different animal populations.

Plants that grow at low elevations in northern regions of North America are often found at high altitudes further south. A person ascending a high mountain may pass through several vegetative zones, each with its own characteristic tree species, before finally reaching timberline and alpine tundra.

Judging the Effects of Environmental Factors —

As a tree new to you is found and identified, it is interesting to think about the environmental factors that enable survival at its present location—and what factors are most likely to be limiting its present distribution and abundance. With seedlings most likely to be affected, could it be shallow soils, snow depth in winter, competition from other plants, excessive soil moisture, drought, lack of soil fertility, excessive soil fertility, fire, insect damage, or what? And what glacial or other geological event might have brought the plant to its present distribution or prevented its spread?

We cannot always answer such questions on the spot. Insights may come, however, as we see other specimens at different locations. It is certain that some combination of natural climatic, soil, biotic, and historic factors has determined the current status of the species and will continue to influence its future welfare. Erosion, over-use, and pollution are human factors that also must be considered.

I. Trees with Needle- or Scale-like Leaves

Forests of the Rocky Mountains display many fine coniferous (needleleaf) trees. All are evergreen *except* the larches (this plate). Conebearing trees are often referred to as *softwoods*, in contrast to broadleaf or *hardwood* trees (Plates 11-42). The many national parks of the United States-Canada border region are especially rich in coniferous species.

1. NEEDLES PINELIKE: Larches

Larches are trees of cold climates that resemble pines in having slender, needlelike foliage and woody cones. Unlike most conifers, however, these trees are *deciduous*, the needles turning bright yellow in autumn and then dropping. Though they are members of the pine family, larches also differ from pines in that they have *many* needles clustered on short *spur branches* and *single* needles on longer shoots. Cones are small with *thin* scales and are *not* prickly.

WESTERN LARCH (TAMARACK) *Larix occidentalis* Nutt

A tall narrow-crowned tree with short branches and sparse foliage. Needles 1"- 1¾" long and twigs *smooth, shiny.* Cones 1"- 1½" long with *pointed* bracts protruding from between the ± papery scales. Trunk often free of branches for half its height with bark red-brown, *thick,* fire-resistant, and in flat plates much like Ponderosa Pine (Plate 4). Height 100'- 180' (240'). The largest of all larches and a valuable timber species. From se. British Columbia and nw. Montana to cen. Oregon and cen. Idaho, mostly between 2000'-8000' elevations.

SUBALPINE LARCH *Larix lyalli* Parl.

An often gnarled and twisted tree on slopes between 5000' and timberline. Needles 1"- 1½" long; twigs *white-woolly.* Cones 1½"- 2" long, with *ragged* protruding bract tips. Bark *thin.* Height 30'- 50' (90'). Ranging across the international border in the North Cascades and again in the Rockies of s. British Columbia /sw. Alberta to cen. Idaho /w. Montana.

TAMARACK (AMERICAN LARCH) *Larix laricina* (DuRoi) K. Koch

With needles ¾"- 1" in length and twigs *hairless,* this larch ranges from cen. Alaska, e. Yukon, and ne. British Columbia east to the Atlantic Ocean. Cones ½"- ¾" long with *no* visible bracts. To 80' tall on wet sites; often stunted or shrubby.

European Larch (*Larix decidua* Mill.), an introduced species sometimes spreading from plantings, has needles and cones both 1"- 1½" long, the latter with pointed bracts *not* visible. The *hairless* twigs and branchlets may *droop.* Trunk bark in large plates. Height to 100'. Mostly uplands.

Plate I

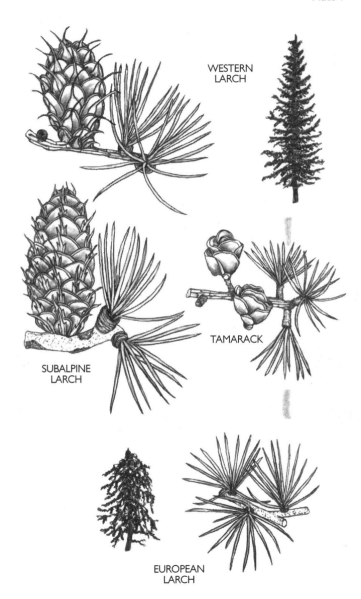

WESTERN
LARCH

SUBALPINE
LARCH

TAMARACK

EUROPEAN
LARCH

PINES: Plates 2–5

Pines have needles, *evergreen,* long, slender, and mostly *clustered.* The familiar female cones are woody, pendent, mostly brown when mature, and with two seeds per cone scale. Seeds often can assist in identification (after one or more cones are dried in a paper bag, those of most species will shake loose). Branches grow in whorls around the trunk, one whorl usually being added at the treetop each year.

Native Americans once ate the seeds of several species and used pine resin to make woven baskets watertight. Pine seeds also are eaten by many birds and small mammals. Twigs and needles are cropped by deer, elk, moose, and other browsing animals, mostly when other foods are scarce. Pine wood is important in the lumber industry.

2. FIVE-NEEDLE PINES: Needles 2½"- 4" Long

The pines of Plates 2 and 3 have *five* slender needles tied in bundles at the base by *short* (under ¹⁄₁₆") papery sheaths. Five-needle pines are called *white* or soft pines because of the color of the wood and the ease with which it is worked. The cones are mostly *not* prickly. Look for them at the tips of high branches and on the ground nearby. Oddly, Arizona (and sometimes Apache) pines are 5-needle *yellow* pines while Chihuahua Pine is a *3-needle* white pine (see Plate 4).

WESTERN WHITE PINE *Pinus monticola* Dougl. ex D. Don
A handsome tree thinly scattered in forests from cen. British Columbia to n. Idaho (also in coastal mountains and the Sierra Nevada). Needles 2 ½"-4" long. Cones *slender, long-stalked,* and *4"-10"* long. Seed ± ³⁄₈" long, the wing *about 1"* in length. The *dark* trunk bark of mature trees is broken into a shallow *checkered* pattern of small squarish pieces. Younger trees have a smoother dark bark with a suggestion of being checkered. To 100'-165' (235') tall mostly in heavy-snowfall areas at middle elevations. Some trees live for 200-500 years. The clear wood has many commercial uses. It is the main source of materials for wooden matches.

SOUTHWESTERN WHITE PINE *Pinus strobiformis* Engelm.
A pine of the Southwest with needles 2 ½"-3" long. Cones *short-stalked, 5"-9"* long, and with scale tips *bent back.* Seeds about ³⁄₈" in length, the wing *lacking* or to ¹⁄₈" long. Bark brownish. Height 60'-80' (100'). Dry slopes, Arizona and s. Colorado to cen. Mexico. *P. reflexa* Engelm. is an older name.

Plate 2

WESTERN
WHITE
PINE

SOUTHWESTERN WHITE
PINE

BARK

3. FIVE-NEEDLE PINES: Needles 1"-2½" Long

In contrast to the 5-needle pines of Plate 2, these white pines have shorter needles and cones. Both cone stalks and scale prickles are short or absent. Mostly at high elevations. Lumber poor.

INTERMOUNTAIN BRISTLECONE PINE *Pinus longaeva* Bailey
The world's longest-living tree, exceeding both Redwood and Giant Sequoia in longevity. Some found to be 4600-5000 years of age. The oldest trees are quite accessible by road in the White Mountains near Bishop, California. Younger trees grow also on high mountains in Nevada and Utah. Needles[1] only *1"-1⅜"* in length but retained for 10-15 (30) years, forming long, bushy, "foxtail" branches. Needles *neither grooved nor sticky*. Cones 3"-4" long with prickles *slender, weak,* and *¹⁄₃₂"-¼"* long. Seed wing ½". (Are aspens, Plate 25, older?)

COLORADO BRISTLECONE PINE *Pinus aristata* Engelm.
Resembling the last species but with foxtail foliage accumulating over 10-17 years, the needles *1"-1⅝'* long, narrowly *grooved,* and often with a *sticky "dandruff"* of tiny resin spheres[1]. Cone prickles are *³⁄₁₆"-⁷⁄₁₆"* in length. At or near timberline in Colorado, n. New Mexico, and n-cen. Arizona. Also called Rocky Mountain Bristlecone Pine.

WHITEBARK PINE *Pinus albicaulis* Engelm.
A timberline tree or windblown shrub with needles 1½"-2½" (3") long and twigs very flexible. Cones *1"-3"* in length, ± *spherical,* dark *purple,* with thick scales that *remain closed.* Most cones are destroyed by birds, chipmunks, or squirrels. Clark Nutcracker, a large black and gray bird of the high country, is especially active in seeking the ⅜"-½" long, *wingless,* nutlike seeds. Squirrel caches are often raided by grizzly bears. Trunk bark in gray to whitish plates but not distinctive. Height 15'-30' (60'). Found at 7000'-12,000' elevations from cen. British Columbia and w-cen. Alberta to w-cen. Idaho and nw. Wyoming. Also coastal-state mountains.

LIMBER PINE *Pinus flexilis* James
Needles and twigs are much like Whitebark Pine. The cones, however, are *elongate, 3"-6"* in length, *light brown,* and with scales that *open readily.* Seeds red-brown, *dark-mottled,* about ½" long with narrow papery wings or none. Though presumably named for its flexible twigs, those of Whitebark Pine also can be twisted into knots. Bark dark, furrowed. Height 35'-50' (80'). Dry ridges, 5000'-12,000' elevations in the Rockies from se. British Columbia/sw. Alberta to se. California and n. New Mexico. Also in the Sierra Nevada.

[1]Needle cross-sections show two resin ducts in *P. longaeva* and one in *P. aristata.*

Plate 3

COLORADO BRISTLECONE PINE

INTER-MOUNTAIN BRISTLECONE PINE

WHITEBARK PINE

SEEDS

LIMBER PINE

4.THREE-NEEDLE PINES

These pines have bundles of *three* needles bound at the base by a long sheath, usually ¼"-1" or more in length. Most pines with 2-3 needles are termed *yellow* or hard pines but pinyon pines (Plate 5) and Chihuahua Pine are exceptions. Cones of yellow pines are usually egg-shaped, *prickly* or thorny, and mostly *short-stalked*. Most species are important for lumber but the wood is pitch-filled and not as suitable for fine work as that of white (soft) pines. Arizona Pine (below) is a 5-needle yellow pine.

PONDEROSA PINE *Pinus ponderosa* Dougl. ex Lawson & C. Lawson
Found throughout the West, a large pine with *5"-10"* needles and sheaths ½"-1" long. Cones mostly *3"-6"* long, *dull*, with prickles mostly *curved out*, total scales *130-140*, and seed wing *1"* long. Mature bark in *yellow* plates faced with *flaky* puzzlelike pieces. Young trunk dark. Height 60'-130' (230'). Sunny sites at 3000'-5000' (9000') elevations. Mule deer browse the twigs; porcupines gnaw the inner bark. **Arizona Pine** [*P. ponderosa* var. *arizonica* (Engelm.) Shaw], a 5-needle form, extends south from se. Arizona and sw. New Mexico. **Washoe Pine** (*P. washoensis* Mason & Stock-well) is similar to Ponderosa Pine but rare in the Sierra of w. Nevada with *4"-6"* needles, *2"-3½"* cones, *160-190* total cone scales, and a ½" seed wing.

JEFFREY PINE *Pinus jeffreyi* Grev. & Balf.
A Sierra pine barely entering w. Nevada. Like Ponderosa Pine but cones are 6"-8" (10") long, *shiny*, with scales *light* brown beneath and prickles mostly *turned in*. Mature *trunk not* flaky, *tightly furrowed*, rosy or *purplish-colored*, and with a pleasant *vanilla odor* (sniff in a furrow). At 6000'-9000' elevations. John Jeffrey was an early Scottish botanical explorer.

Near the Mexican border: Chihuahua Pine [*P. leiophylla* var. *chihuahuana* (Engelm.) Shaw], though a member of the white pine group, has clusters of three *thin* needles 2½"-4" long with *short* (⅟₁₆") basal sheaths. Twigs *slim*. Cones 1½"-3" long, *long-stalked*, and *not* prickly; seed ⅛", wing ⁵⁄₁₆". From e-cen. Arizona and sw. New Mexico to cen. Mexico. Pronounced chee-WAH-wah. With a similar range, **Apache Pine** (*P. engelmannii* Carr.) has *8"-15"* needles (sometimes in 2s or 5s), *1"-1½"* needle sheaths, *thumb-wide* twigs, and *4"-6"* prickly cones. Seed ⁵⁄₁₆"; wing 1". **Mexican Pinyon** (*P. cembroides* Zucc.) has *stout* needles, *slender* twigs, and wingless nuts. Both needles and cones are only *1"-2½"* in length, the cones *not* prickly. From se. Arizona/sw. New Mexico/w-cen. Texas to cen. Mexico. **Parry Pinyon** (*P. quadrifolia* Parl. ex Sudw.) has 1"-1½" needles, (3-) *4* per cluster and cones 1½"-2½", ± prickly. Riverside /San Diego counties, sw. California, and Baja California.

Plate 4

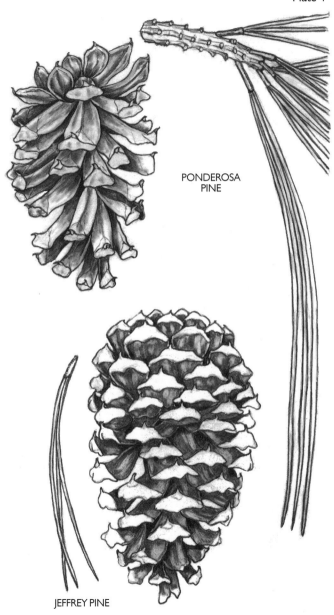

PONDEROSA
PINE

JEFFREY PINE

5. PINES w/ONE or TWO NEEDLES per BUNDLE

Singleleaf Pine usually has only one needle per "cluster"; three other pines regularly have paired needles. Pinyon pines have short needle-sheaths, indicating a white pine relationship. Ponderosa and Apache pines (Plate 4) sometimes may have two-needle foliage.

SINGLELEAF PINYON *Pinus monophylla* Torr. & Frém.

Easily recognized by its *single* needle and offering tasty nuts to eat, this is a good pine to know. Needle thick, *spine-tipped*, grayish, and 1"-2½" long, rarely in twos. Cones 2"-3" long, stout, *thornless*, soon *falling*. Nuts about three-fourths of an inch long and ± *wingless*. Especially good when roasted, the nuts are much prized by people who find them before they are eaten by birds or rodents. Grows to 40' in height, mainly on arid sites. Great Basin region to s. California. The state tree of Nevada.

LODGEPOLE PINE *Pinus contorta* Dougl. ex Loud.

Lodgepole Pine is a *narrow-crowned* tree with *yellow-green* needles only *1"-2" (3")* in length and sheaths just ⅛"-⅛" (³⁄₁₆") long. Cones 1"-2" long, often *persisting* on the tree, the scales *thin* and *prickly*. Seeds ³⁄₁₆"; wing ½". Mature trunk bark mostly *thin, scaly, cornflakelike*. Height 60'-100' (115'). At 3000'-11,000' elevations from se. Alaska and cen. Yukon to s. California and s. Colorado. Often grows in dense stands ("like hair on a dog's back") especially after a forest fire. Seeds are eaten by squirrels and grouse, twigs are browsed by deer, the inner bark is gnawed by porcupines. Logs and lumber much used in home construction. Native Americans once used the trunks of saplings to support their teepee lodges.

JACK PINE *Pinus banksiana* Lamb.

An often-straggly tree with both 2-needle clusters and cones only *1"-1½"* long, the cones strongly *bulged* on one side and long-held on branches. Seed ⅛"; wing ⅜". Seeds released mostly as a result of fires. Height ±15'-40'. Distributed west across Canada and the northern United States, reaching the Rockies in Alberta and ne. British Columbia. May hybridize with Lodgepole Pine.

TWO-NEEDLE PINYON *Pinus edulis* Engelm.

A short, round-topped, nut pine of the cen. and s. Rockies. Needles *paired*, ¾"-2" long, dark green, sharp but *not* spiny. Cones 1"-2" in length, ± spherical, with *thick*, blunt, *thornless* scales and half-inch, wingless, edible nuts. Height 15'-20' (50'). Reportedly single-needled in cen. Arizona. The state tree of New Mexico.

Plate 5

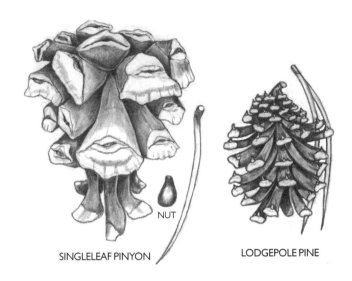

SINGLELEAF PINYON

NUT

LODGEPOLE PINE

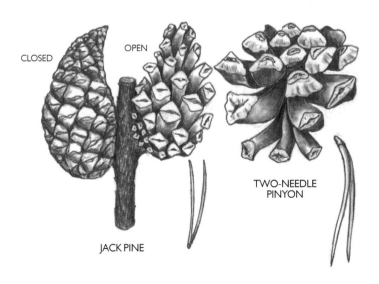

CLOSED

OPEN

JACK PINE

TWO-NEEDLE
PINYON

6. NEEDLES on WOODY PEGS: Spruces

Spruces have *single* needles on *small, stout, woody pegs* (seen best on dead twigs/branchlets) and *drop* upon drying. Hemlocks (Plate 8) have only weak needle-pegs. In our species, needles are mostly *4-sided, stiff, pointed,* and grow all around the twig. Twigs mostly *hairless* (remove needles and use lens). Cones brown and woody with *papery* scales and *no* prickles. Trunk bark *brown-scaly.*

Spruce wood is soft, light, and straight-grained. It is a principal source of pulp for making paper. The inner bark has been pulverized and added to flour in bad times. Spruce beer reportedly can be made from fermented needles and twigs boiled with honey. Several species are used in landscaping.

ENGELMANN SPRUCE *Picea engelmannii* Parry ex Engelm.
  The principal spruce of inland mountains from cen. British Columbia to n. California and s. New Mexico. Needles dark- to blue-green, ± flexible, only moderately sharp. Twigs mostly *hairy.* Cones 1"-2" (3") long, with scale tips *ragged.* Height 80'-100' (180'). A major lumber tree, sometimes with resonant logs. George Engelmann was a 19th century physician and botanist. See Blue Spruce.

BLUE SPRUCE *Picea pungens* Engelm.
  Much like Engelmann Spruce and often difficult to distinguish from it. Needles *stiff* and *sharp,* twigs *hairless,* cones *2"-4"* long with scale tips *ragged.* Foliage green to blue-green, seldom as blue as cultivated varieties. Bark tends to be *darker,* thicker, and more furrowed than that of Engelmann Spruce. E-cen. Idaho /w. Wyoming to se. Arizona/s. New Mexico. State tree of Colorado and Utah.

WHITE SPRUCE *Picea glauca* (Moench) Voss
  A pyramidal tree with twigs *hairless* and needles yellow-to-blue-green, $3/8"$-$3/4"$ long. Cones *1½"-2"* in length, the scale tips *smoothly rounded.* Cones *not* retained long on the tree. Height 50'-60'. Upland tundras and forests. Trees may live for 200 years. Crossbills and red squirrels eat the seeds; porcupines strip the inner bark; deer, moose, and bighorn sheep may browse the twigs. White and Black spruces are cold-hardy species that grow south from the limit of trees across Alaska and Canada to the lower 48 states. This species grows south over *most* of British Columbia, reaching nw. Montana. See Black Spruce.

BLACK SPRUCE *Picea mariana* (Mill.) BSP
  Closely resembles White Spruce but with twigs *hairy* (use lens) and needles green to blue-green, only $1/4"$-$7/16"$ long. Cones $3/4"$-$1¼"$ *long,* the scale tips *ragged.* Cones *tend to remain on the tree.* Height 25'-30'. Bogs and wet tundras. Transcontinental in the north, ranging southward over *northern* portions British Columbia and the prairie provinces.

22

Plate 6

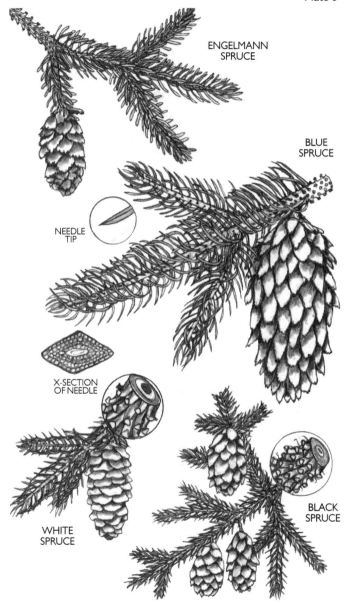

ENGELMANN
SPRUCE

BLUE
SPRUCE

NEEDLE
TIP

X-SECTION
OF NEEDLE

BLACK
SPRUCE

WHITE
SPRUCE

7. NEEDLES ± FLAT on THIN STALKS

The needles of these trees are *white-banded* beneath (see also Plate 8) and attached to the twigs by almost-hairlike *thin stalks*. (Note: whitish markings on conifer needles disappear from weathered or dried specimens; it is best to examine *fresh twig-end foliage*.) Except for Mountain Hemlock, needles of these trees are *flat* and *in flat sprays*. Cones are brown, dry, and *pendent*. Unlike true firs (Plate 8), the cones do not shed their scales. Hemlock needles are on weak pegs, making dead twigs *slightly* rough (see spruces, Plate 6). Often hemlocks can be recognized at a distance by the *drooping* 1'-3' long top leader shoot (see also Western Redcedar, Plate 9).

COMMON DOUGLAS-FIR *Pseudotsuga menziesii* (Mirb.) Franco
Best field marks: twigs *drooping* markedly and *3-pointed bracts* protruding between the woody cone scales (look for cones on and beneath the tree). Needles ¾"-1½" long. Plucked twigs show *smooth circular* leaf scars as in true firs, but buds are sharply *pointed*. Topmost shoot *erect*. Trunk bark dark and grooved. Height 80'-100' (300'). An important lumber tree distributed throughout western mountains, north nearly to se. Alaska. Named for David Douglas, an early Scottish botanist, but found by Archibald Menzies one of Douglas' countrymen.

WESTERN HEMLOCK *Tsuga heterophylla* (Raf.) Sarg.
An attractive shade-tolerant tree with needles only ¼"-¾" long and of *different lengths*. Cones delicate, only ¾"-1" long. Trunks brown to gray with scaly ridges. Height 125'-160' (200'). On Pacific slopes from s. Alaska to n. California and again at low to middle elevations in the Rocky Mountains of se. British Columbia/sw. Alberta/n. Idaho. Native Americans made flour from the inner bark in emergencies.

MOUNTAIN HEMLOCK *Tsuga mertensiana* (Bong.) Carr.
Needles only ¼"-¾" long, ± *rounded* in cross-section, and *spreading starlike in all directions*. *All* surfaces are whitened, the tree appearing blue-green. Cones 1½"-2" (3") long, brown, narrow. Height 30'-100' (150'). Deep snow areas and high elevations in the Rocky Mountain region of se. British Columbia/n. Idaho, also in coastal ranges from s. Alaska to Puget Sound, and south in the Cascades/Sierra Nevada.

PACIFIC YEW *Taxus brevifolia* Nutt.
An often shrubby species with needles $\frac{1}{2}$"-1" long, green on *both* sides, pointed, and with bases *extending along* the *green* twigs. Mature fruits *bright red*, juicy, with an open end revealing a dark seed. Height 25'-50' (75'). Coastal slopes and again in the se. British Columbia/n. Idaho/n. Oregon/ne. Washington/ nw. Montana area. Valued by Native Americans for making bows. Bark chemicals useful in treating some cancers.

Plate 7

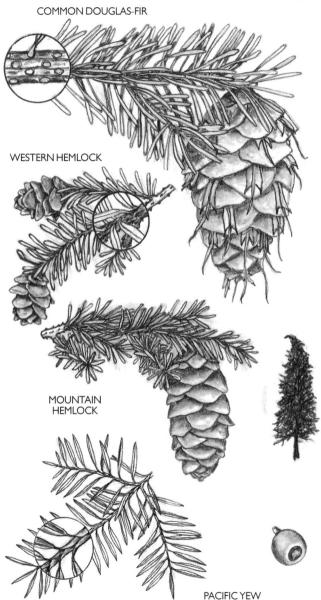

COMMON DOUGLAS-FIR

WESTERN HEMLOCK

MOUNTAIN
HEMLOCK

PACIFIC YEW

8. NEEDLES FLAT, NOT STALKED: True Firs

True firs (genus *Abies*) are beautiful, steeple-shaped trees that thrive mainly in snowy climates. Needles are single *without* thin stalks (but see White Fir). Our firs have needles *flat*, *blunt*, and *double white-striped* beneath (see *fresh* twig-end foliage). Though true firs have smooth twigs with *circular* leaf scars like Douglas-firs, the buds of true firs are *rounded*, not pointed. The trunk of young trees is gray, mostly with resin-filled *blisters*. Older trunks are darker and usually furrowed. The topmost shoot is *erect*.

Fir cones stand *erect*, mostly ripening from green to purple. Scales are *thick*, *fleshy*, and *soon fall*, leaving a slim upright stalk. Whole cones often absent but sometimes are nearby where cut by squirrels before they mature. Bracts *hidden* between the cone scales.

ROCKY MOUNTAIN SUBALPINE FIR *Abies bifolia* Murray
Branches have needles mostly directed upward, *hiding* the twigs from above. Needles are ¾"-1¼" long, whitened *both above and below*, with a *single white stripe above*. Needle tips rounded or notched. Twigs sometimes hairy; fresh leaf scar edges tan and basal bud scale edges smooth. Mature cones 2½"-4" long. Trunk bark grayish, smooth when young. Height 20'-100' (130'). Ranges in the Rockies from se. Yukon and sw. Northwest Territories to Arizona/New Mexico. Corkbark Fir [var. *arizonica* (Merriam) Lemmon] occurs southward from s. Colorado with soft whitish bark. The Subalpine Fir of coastal states/provinces, with leaf scar edges reddish and bud scales ragged, retains the older name *A. lasiocarpa* (Hook.) Nutt.[2]

GRAND FIR *Abies grandis* (Dougl. ex D. Don) Lindl.
A handsome tree with needles arranged *in flat sprays*, the twigs *clearly visible* from above. Needles of *different lengths*, ¾"-1" (2") long, mostly over ⅟₁₆" wide, *medium-green*, grooved above, *white-lined beneath*, and *notch-tipped* (use lens). Height 150'- 200' (250'). At low elevations from se. British Columbia and nw. Montana to e. Oregon and cen. Idaho, also coastal forests. Fast-growing and tolerant of shade. Wood reported to repel insects. May live 300 years or so.

WHITE FIR *Abies concolor* (Gord. & Glend.) Hildebr.
Like Grand Fir but the needles mostly curve upward in a *shallow U-shape*, all of *about equal* length. Needles *1¼"-2¼"* (3") long, *blue-green*, ± *white-powdered*, often ± *narrowed* at the base, tips *rounded*, with two *pale green lines* beneath. Cones green, 3"-5" long. Height 100'-180' (210'). Low and middle elevations from sw. Oregon, se. Idaho, and cen. Colorado into Mexico. Intergrades with Grand Fir are reported.

[2] *Abies bifolia* is not always recognized as different.

Plate 8

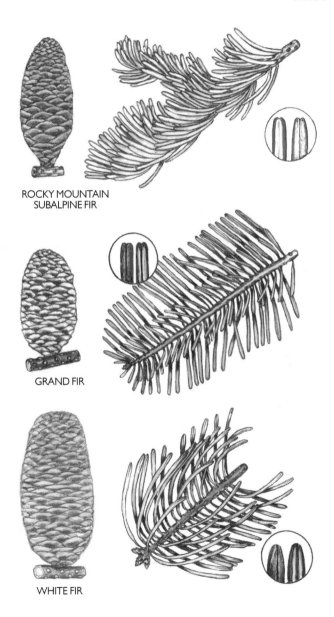

ROCKY MOUNTAIN
SUBALPINE FIR

GRAND FIR

WHITE FIR

9. LEAVES ALL SCALELIKE

Mostly conebearing trees whose twigs are covered by tiny blunt leaf scales and whose fruits are woody cones. Tamarisks[3] differ.

WESTERN RED CEDAR *Thuja plicata* Donn ex D. Don

A beautiful and valuable tree of coastal and inland mountains. Twigs densely covered by small, *scalelike,* mostly aromatic leaves arranged in *flat sprays.* Leaves ⅟₁₆"-⅛" long, *broadly whitened* beneath in a so-called butterfly pattern (use lens). Gland dots *lacking.* Foliage *droops* or forms inverted Vs. Cones *slender, erect,* ½"-¾" long, with 8-10 scales. Trunk red-brown, *vertically grooved,* often with basal buttresses. Leader shoot short, but may droop or lean (see hemlocks, Plate 7). Height 60'-130' (180'). Near the coast from se. British Columbia to ne. Washington/n. Idaho/nw. Montana. Lumber durable. Native Americans made the trunks into war canoes holding up to 40 people. They also fashioned ropes, nets, blankets, baskets, and roof thatch from the fibrous bark.

INCENSE-CEDAR *Calocedrus decurrens* (Torr.) Florin

A beautiful, large, cone-shaped tree whose smooth *glossy* foliage scales are *long* (to ½") and arranged in unique *vase-shaped whorls* (use lens). Gland dots are *absent.* Crushed foliage has a *pleasant* odor. Cones ¾"-1" long, *slim,* bell-shaped, *pendent,* with six brown scales, two of them short. Bark thick, red-brown. In the Sierra, reaching east to w. Nevada. Formerly *Libocedrus.*

CYPRESSES (this plate) and Junipers (Plate 10) are quite similar in general appearance. Both have blunt leaf scales under ¼" long, often aromatic, and mostly showing central *gland-dots* (use lens). These leafscales hug twigs that are ± *4-sided,* mostly about ⅟₁₆" thick, and *not* in flat sprays. Cypresses have *only* scalelike leaves while junipers tend *also* to have small, sharp, awl-shaped needles present. Cypresses, with both sexes on the *same* tree, usually have *woody, brown, spherical* cones *present.* Juniper cones are solid, *hard-fleshy,* more or less spherical, either blue or red-brown when mature (often with a whitish powder), and often scarce (see Plate 10). **Arizona Cypress** (*Cupressus arizonica* Greene) is the only cypress in our area. It has 4-sided twigs that *branch at wide angles.* From se. Arizona to w. Texas into Mexico. Trees with smooth reddish bark are often separated as *C. glabra* Sudw. and called Smooth Cypress.

[3] **Tamarisks** are exotic non-conifers with small *true flowers* and tiny *juniperlike* leaves. Twigs are cylindrical rather than 4-sided and have no resinous odor. French Tamarisk (*Tamarix gallica* L.) is *deciduous,* spreading in some areas and often called Salt-cedar. Athel Tamarisk [*T. aphylla* (L.) Karst.], densely *evergreen,* is established locally from s. Texas to s. Calif. See junipers Pl. 10.

Plate 9

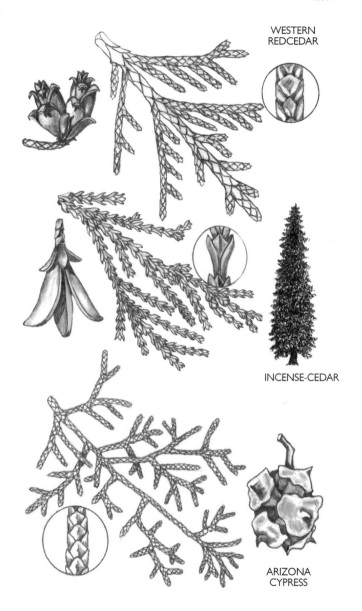

WESTERN
REDCEDAR

INCENSE-CEDAR

ARIZONA
CYPRESS

10. LEAVES both SCALELIKE and AWL-SHAPED: Junipers

Unlike cypresses (Plate 9), junipers mostly display small, sharp, awl-shaped needles *in addition* to scalelike foliage not in flat sprays. Pointed needles occur mainly near twig ends. Scaly leaves mostly show a *gland-dot* (use lens). Twigs mostly about 1/16" thick. See also Tamarisks, Plate 9.

Junipers bear *hard-fleshy* and ± spherical fruits, considered to be cones with fused scales. When mature, they are mostly 1/4"-1/2" in diameter and *either* blue and juicy, or red-brown and dry. Fruits are often scarce, falling when ripe and also eaten by wildlife. The sexes are mostly separate, too; female specimens must be located to secure cones. Fruits of one or two sizes, maturing over one or two years.

Most junipers are under 40' tall and grow on dry sites. The dried, shreddy bark of most species is good for starting fires. Fruits of some species were eaten by Native Americans and early settlers.

ROCKY MOUNTAIN JUNIPER *Juniperus scopulorum* Sarg.
A widely distributed juniper with twigs ± *threadlike* (only about 1/32" thick), ± 4-sided, and *drooping.* Leaf scales bluish to *dark* green, ± *long-pointed,* usually with a gland. Cones *blue, juicy,* *2-seeded,* and of *two* sizes. From e-cen. British Columbia to Arizona and New Mexico. Bighorn sheep browse the twigs.

ONE-SEED JUNIPER *Juniperus monosperma* (Engelm.) Sarg.
Ranging from s. Utah and s. Colorado to Mexico, this juniper has wider (± 1/16") twigs and leaves *gray-green.* Fruits are *blue,* single-seeded, and of *one* size.

UTAH JUNIPER *Juniperus osteosperma* (Torr.) Little
Lacking leaf gland dots, this tree has only one (rarely two) seeds. Leaf scales are *yellow*-green and *short-pointed.* Mature cones dry, *red-brown,* and of either *1 or 2* sizes. Distributed from se. Idaho and s. Montana to Arizona and nw. New Mexico. Reported to be the most common tree in Utah and Nevada.

WESTERN (Sierra) JUNIPER *Juniperus occidentalis* Hook.
A juniper with leaf scales *gray*-green, *not* long-pointed. Fruits *blue-black,* juicy, of *two* sizes. Mostly west of our area, from cen. Washington/sw. Idaho to s. California/w. Nevada.

Common Juniper (*J. communis* L.) has *only* whitened awl-shaped needles in *whorls of three.* Northern. Rarely tree size.

Junipers of Mexican border areas: **Alligator Juniper** (*J. deppeana* Steud.) ranges southward from cen. Arizona, cen. New Mexico, and w. Texas with a *checkered* trunk, leaf scales *blue-green* and *long-pointed,* the fruits reddish and of *two* sizes. **Weeping Juniper** (*J. flaccida* Schlecht.) of sw. Texas and nearby Mexico has branches *strongly drooping* and *one-size* reddish fruits. **More junipers** on Plate 39.

Plate 10

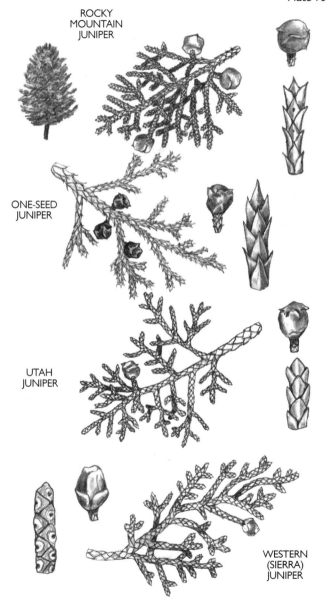

ROCKY
MOUNTAIN
JUNIPER

ONE-SEED
JUNIPER

UTAH
JUNIPER

WESTERN
(SIERRA)
JUNIPER

II. Trees with Opposite Compound Leaves

In contrast to the needleleaf species of Plates 1-10, most other trees of our region are *broadleaf* plants with either compound or simple foliage. Forty-four of these trees have *compound* leaves. Foliage of the eight species on Plates 11-12 are *opposite* while the leaves of the 36 trees of Plates 15-20 are *alternate*. When leaves are absent, the bare twigs of all opposite-leaved species (Plates 11-14) may need to be compared. See also the Key to Trees in Leafless Condition (pp. 96-98). When leaves have only three leaflets, see also Plates 12 and 20. *Be sure not to mistake the leaflets of a compound leaf for the blades of simple leaves* (Figure 1, page 8). Trees that have spur branches crowded with leaf scars (Figure 2, page 9) often appear to have opposite leaf scars. Among our truly opposite-leaved species, however, only Desert-olive Forestiera (Plate 12) has spur branches.

I I. LEAFLETS w/ UNEVEN BASES: Elderberries

Elderberries are trees or shrubs whose leaflets have *uneven* bases and whose twigs are thick but *weak*, containing *wide* pith. Buds are *obviously* scaly, a central terminal bud is *lacking*, and *lines* connect the paired leaf scars. Bundle scars are 3-7. Tiny, white, summer flowers and *small, juicy, several-seeded* fruits occur in ± *flat-topped* twig-end clusters 2"-8" across. The blue to black fruits may have a *whitish coating*. Though reported to contain hydrocyanic acid, they are reported often to be cooked into jam or jelly. The two species are often combined as varieties of *S. mexicana* Presl.

BLUE ELDERBERRY *Sambucus caerulea* Raf.
> A widespread western elderberry. Leaves 5"-8" long with *3-9* short- to *long-pointed* leaflets. Leaflets *2"-6"* in length, *hairless*, and mostly *fine-toothed*. Side leaflets have stalks ¼"-½" long. The dark but white-powdered fruits display a beautiful *sky-blue* color. Though mostly shrubby, some plants become 25' tall. Widespread from s. British Columbia to n. Mexico at elevations to 10,000'.

VELVET ELDERBERRY *Sambucus velutina* Durand & Hilgard
> From California east to w-cen. Nevada and nw. Arizona, this elderberry has leaves with only *3-5* leaflets. Leaflets *short-pointed, velvet-hairy, fine-toothed*, and only *1"-3"* long. Stalks of side leaflets are *lacking* or under ³⁄₁₆" long. Fruits *blackish*. To 20' tall on slopes at 3000'-8000' elevations. Native Americans often favored this species for making fires. They used a dry half-inch branch as a spindle, spinning the wood between their hands. The base of the spindle, or drill, was forced into a small pit in a flat piece of dry cottonwood or juniper root and surrounded by shredded tinder. The spindle was rotated rapidly until friction caused smoke and, finally, flame to ensue.

Plate 11

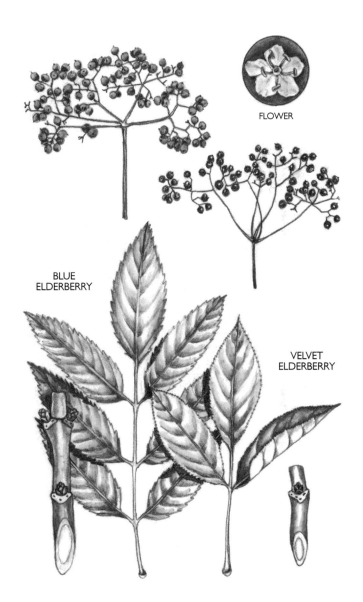

FLOWER

BLUE
ELDERBERRY

VELVET
ELDERBERRY

12. LEAFLET BASES EVEN: Ashes/Ashleaf Maple

Ash leaves have 3-9 leaflets mostly *fine-toothed*, long-pointed, and bases *even*. Buds rounded, mostly brown with a smooth-granular surface, the central end bud *present*. Leaf scars shield-shaped with *many* bundle scars (use lens). Twigs *strong* with pith *narrow* and small branches mostly opposite. Flowers small, dark, *clustered*, mostly *without* petals, in early spring usually ahead of the leaves. Fruits *dry*, one-seeded, with a *single* wing like the blade of a canoe paddle. Trunk mostly gray, *fine-fissured*. Singleleaf Ash is on Plate 14. Velvet Ash, at bottom of page, ranges north to sw. Utah. European Ash (*F. excelsior* L.), sometimes planted, has leaflets 7-13 and buds *black*. **Ashleaf Maple** is *large-toothed* and usually *trifoliate* with leaf scars *meeting in raised points*. Western Mountain Maple (Plate 13) sometimes may display three-parted leaves.

GREEN ASH *Fraxinus pennsylvanicus* Marsh.

> Reaching west to the Rockies of w. Alberta/w. Montana/Utah, this eastern ash has leaves *8"-12"* long with 5-9 leaflets whose short stalks have *narrow wings*. Fruits 1"-2" in length, *not* winged to the seed base. Seed *plump*, *very slender*, pointed at *both* ends. Moist soils. Wood important in making canoe paddles. Specimens with hairy twigs were once called Red Ash.

ASHLEAF MAPLE (BOX-ELDER) *Acer negundo* L.

> Unlike ashes, leaf teeth are *large and coarse* (occasionally none), twigs green or purple, leaf scars *narrow*, *meeting in raised points*, bundle scars *3* (-5), buds *white-hairy*, flowers *green*; and fruits *paired* maple "keys" (see Plate 13). Trunk bark *dark*. Height 50'-70'. Ranging west to w. Alberta/nw. Montana and across the cen. and s. Rockies. The only regional maple with leaves always compound. The sap can be made into syrup. Foliage looks like Poison-oak [*Toxicodendron diversilobum* (Torrey & Gray) Greene] but its leaves are alternate not opposite. Wood is used for boxes but tree is not related to elders.

Ashes of the Southwest: Found north to sw. Utah, **Velvet Ash** (*F. velutina* Torr.) has leaflets *long-pointed* at both ends and *wavy-toothed* near the tip. Fruit wing *half* as long as the *plump* seed. **Fragrant Ash** (*F. cuspidata* Torr.) ranges south from n. Arizona and w. Texas with *coarse-toothed* foliage and *fragrant* white flowers. Fruits winged to the *base*; seed *flat*. **Chihuahua Ash** (*F. papillosa* Lingelsh.) occurs south from se. Arizona with leaflets ± *whitish* beneath and the fruit wing extending to the *base* of a *flat* seed. In sw. Texas and n. Mexico, **Gregg Ash** (*F. greggii* Gray) has leaves only *1"-2½"* long, the midrib *winged* and seed *plump*. **Goodding Ash** (*F. gooddingii* Little) of se. Ariz. is similar but with seed *flat*. **Lowell Ash** (*F. lowellii* Sarg.), of n. and cen. Arizona, has twigs *4-lined* or 4-angled.

Plate 12

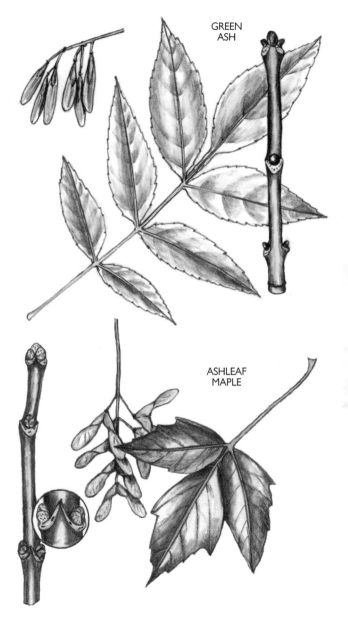

GREEN
ASH

ASHLEAF
MAPLE

III. Trees with Opposite Simple Leaves

Species with opposite compound leafage were covered in Section II (Plates 11-12); the seven trees with opposite *simple* leaves are discussed in this Section (Plates 13-14). When leafless, plates of all trees with opposite leaf scars (Plates 11-14) must be compared. Desert-willow (Plate 33) and buckthorns (Plates 37, 39) may have some leaves opposite.

13. OPPOSITE LEAVES FAN-LOBED: Maples

The only trees with opposite *lobed* foliage in our area are maples, and only they have the *paired, dry, winged* fruits called *keys* (for Ashleaf Maple, see Plate 12). Leafstalks of maples are *long*, twigs are slender and mostly red-brown, buds are mostly hairless and pointed, bundle scars are *three*, and flowers are in *umbrella-shaped* groups. Small trees to 40' tall. Autumn foliage is colorful and the springtime sap can be boiled into a sweet syrup. Arizona Sycamore and California Fremontia (Plate 23) as well as White Poplar (Plate 25) have *alternate* leaves often maplelike.

WESTERN MOUNTAIN MAPLE *Acer glabrum* Torr.

A shrub or small tree with leaves *4"-7"* long, *3-5* lobed, and with leaf teeth *many* and *sharp*. Foliage sometimes divided into *three coarse-toothed leaflets* (see Plate 12). Buds with *two* scales. Flowers May-July. Each fruit *¾"-1"* long; the paired fruits *V-angled* at about 45°, August-September. Distributed through the western mountains from se. Alaska and e-cen. British Columbia to n. Mexico. Also known as Rocky Mountain Maple and Douglas Maple. Twigs are browsed by deer, mountain sheep, and cottontail rabbits; seeds are eaten by squirrels and many kinds of birds. In winter, dogwoods (Plate 14) also show two bud scales but twig leaf scars are raised and fruits are fleshy.

CANYON MAPLE *Acer grandidentatum* Nutt.

A small-foliaged maple with leaves *2"-4½"* long and equally wide. Leaf teeth *rounded*, large, relatively *few*, and widely-spaced. Buds mostly *4-scaled*. Flowers April-May. Single fruit *½"-1"* long, in *U-shaped* pairs, June-September. Truly a tree of the Rocky Mountains, ranging from s-cen. Montana, se. Idaho, and w. Wyoming to se. Arizona, s-cen. Texas, and Mexico. Also known as Bigtooth Maple, a translation of the scientific name. Sometimes tapped for its sweet sap and called Sugar Maple, though that name is better reserved for the eastern *A. saccharum* that yields the maple sugar and maple syrup of commerce (two of the few foods native to North America).

Plate 13

WESTERN
MOUNTAIN
MAPLE

CANYON
MAPLE

14. OPPOSITE LEAVES NOT LOBED

Except for Singleleaf Ash, these trees lack leaf teeth.

SINGLELEAF ASH *Fraxinus anomala* S. Watson

An unusual ash mainly with only *one* leaflet (occasionally 2-3). Leaves 2"-3" long, hairless, often *almost circular*, with *blunt* teeth or none. Twigs *4-lined* or 4-angled; bundle scars many. Flowers tiny, greenish, *lacking* petals, spring. Fruits dry, ½"-¾" long, seed flattened, winged to the base, summer. Mountains from Utah and w. Colorado to se. California and s. Arizona. Common in Zion and Grand Canyon national parks. Lowell Ash (Plate 12) also has 4-lined twigs.

SILVER BUFFALOBERRY *Shepherdia argentea* Nutt.

A shrub or small tree with *silver-scaly* foliage, twigs, and buds. Leaves *1"-2½"* long, ± leathery, and bases *V-shaped*. Twigs often *thorn-tipped*; bud scales *2*; bundle scar *1*. Flowers small, green, without petals, April-June; fruits small, orange-red, fleshy, July-Sept. To 15' in height. Ranging west across the plains to sw. Alberta/w. Montana/Wyoming, locally to w. Nevada, sw. Utah, and cen. New Mexico; absent from parts of the Great Basin. Fruits said to be useful for jelly. Russian-olive (Plate 33), a widely-planted and ± thorny imported tree, also has silvery foliage and twigs but its leaves are alternate.

RED-OSIER DOGWOOD *Cornus sericea* L.

This continent-wide and mostly-shrubby species, like all dogwoods, has oval leaves with lateral veins that tend to *follow the leaf edges*. Leaves 2"-4" long, ± hairy, with *4-7* pairs of side veins. Twigs *bright red*, with leaf scars *raised*, buds *2-scaled*, bundle scars *three*, and pith *white*. Flowers small, *white*, in flat-topped clusters, May-July; fruits small, *white*, fleshy, July-December. To 26' tall. Moist sites. Twigs browsed by deer, elk, moose, cottontail rabbits, and snowshoe hares; fruits eaten by ruffed and sharptail grouse, bandtail pigeons, and other birds. Also called American Dogwood. Formerly named *C. stolonifera* Michx.

BUTTONBUSH *Cephalanthus occidentalis* L.

A widespread shrub or small tree of wet soils usually with some leaves in *whorls* of three or four. Buds ± scaly and mostly *buried* in the bark. Bundle scar *single*. Pith *brown*. Flowers small, white, in tight *long-stemmed* balls at twig ends. Fruits *dry*, in *spherical* heads ¾"-1" wide. Height sometimes to 20'-30'. Transcontinental, but in our area mainly Arizona.

Desert-olive Forestiera (*Forestiera pubescens* Nutt.), a *near-evergreen* shrub or small tree of s. Arizona, has leaves 1"-1½" long, ⅛"-¼" wide, *blunt*, *wedge-based*, and edges rolled. Leaves may be clustered on *spur branches*. Bundle scar *one*. Charles LaForestier was a French naturalist of the 1800s. Also known as *F. phillyreoides* (Benth.) Torr.

Plate 14

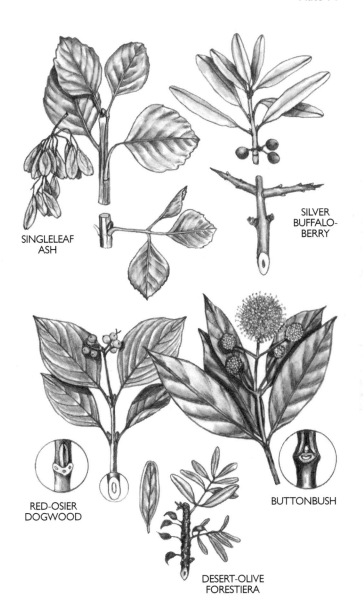

SINGLELEAF ASH

SILVER BUFFALO-BERRY

RED-OSIER DOGWOOD

BUTTONBUSH

DESERT-OLIVE FORESTIERA

IV. Trees with Alternate Compound Leaves

The trees of Plates 15-20 have alternate feather-compound foliage (see Figure 1, page 8). [Trees with fan-compound leaves grow in other regions.] Thorny trees are on Plates 15-17.

15. TREES THORNY, LEAVES ONCE-COMPOUND

All of these trees are legumes with *pealike* blossoms and *pod* fruits.

NEW MEXICO LOCUST *Robinia neomexicana* A. Gray

A small tree, the leaves *4"-10"* long with 9-21 smooth-edged, *bristle-tipped* leaflets. Leaflets ¾"-1½" long and ½"-1" wide. Twigs hairy or not, the *paired* thorns ¼"-½" long flanking the leaf scars. Buds *break through* the leaf scars in spring. Bundle scars 3. Spur branches lacking. Flowers *pink-purple*, in drooping *2"-4"* clusters, spring; fruit pods 2"-6" in length, *brown-hairy*, autumn or later. Height to 25'. Mountains, from se. Nevada and cen. Colorado to w. Texas and n. Mexico. As in many other legumes, root nodules contain bacteria that convert atmospheric nitrogen into soil-enriching compounds. Deer browse the twigs; wild turkeys and other birds eat the seeds. Native Americans ate the fresh flowers and cooked the seeds.

BLACK LOCUST *Robinia pseudoacacia* L.

Like New Mexico Locust but with leaves *8"-14"* long, the leaflets *smoothly blunt-tipped* and occasionally fine-toothed. Flowers *white*, in clusters *4"-6"* long; fruit pods *hairless*. Trunk dark with thick, intersecting ridges. Height 70'-100'. Though native to eastern North America, Black Locust is spreading rapidly in temperate zones around the world; it may be encountered anywhere in our area. Makes durable fence posts. Seeds and bark listed as poisonous to livestock and people.

In s. Arizona near the international boundary: Desert Ironwood (*Olneya tesota* A.Gray) usually presents a dense mass of thick, gray-green, *evergreen* leaves, each 2"-4" long with 8-20 blunt, fine-hairy leaflets ½"-¾" in length. Twigs greenish and hairless, often with thorns *both* paired and single, and sometimes with small spur branches. Flowers lavender, each ½" long, in clusters to 1½" in length, May-June. Fruit pods 1"-3" long, hairy, and narrowed between the 1-6 black seeds. Trunk bark gray-shreddy. Height 25'-30'. Desert washes and depressions, se. California/sw. Arizona. One of the heaviest American woods; fresh wood will not float. Outstanding for firewood and becoming scarce in consequence. Native Americans made arrowheads of the wood, ate the flowers, and made flour of the seeds. Intolerant of cold. Also called Tesota (teh-SO-tah) and Palo de Hierro (PAH-lo-day-YAIR-oh), Spanish for Ironwood. **Southwestern Coralbean** (*Erythrina flabelliformis* Kearn.) of se. Arizona/sw. New Mexico has leaves with 3 triangular, toothless, 2"-4" leaflets. Twigs stout, ± hairy; thorns single, ⅛"-¼" long.

Plate 15

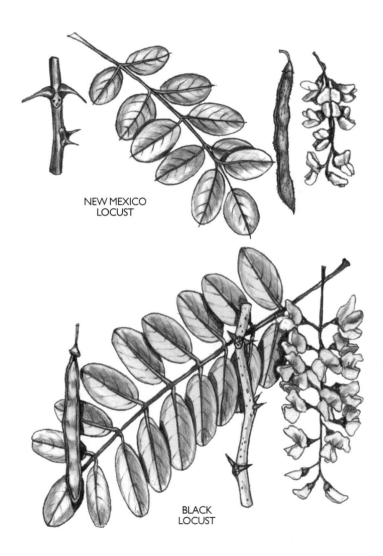

NEW MEXICO
LOCUST

BLACK
LOCUST

16. THORNS PAIRED, LEAVES TWICE-COMPOUND

These are trees of arid and semi-arid soils, mainly in the Southwest. Leaves are divided into *major* leaflets and again into *minor* leaflets (Figure 1, page 8). Thorns *straight* or slightly curved. Spur branches *present*, leaflets *blunt* and *smooth-edged*, flowers in slender clusters, fruits are *pods*. Mesquites have only *one pair* of major leaflets (rarely 2-3 pairs). See also Roemer Catclaw (Plate 17).

HONEY MESQUITE *Prosopis glandulosa* Torr.

A small tree or shrub with leaves *5"-10"* long. Each of the two major leaflets has 10-20 pairs of minor leaflets ⅛"-¼" wide and ¾"-1½" in length. Spur branches are about ⅜" long and *obvious* on the branchlets. Thorns, occasionally single, are ±1" in length. Flowers white to *pale yellow*, clusters 2"-7" long, April-July; fruit pods cylindrical, brown, *4"-10"* long, and ± *beaded*. Trunk brown, often dark. Height to 20'. Rangelands, se. California and sw. Utah to n-cen. Texas and most of Mexico. Once confined to streamsides by grassland wildfires but heavy grazing and fire control have enabled its spread into uplands. Useful for fence posts, firewood, and charcoal. Cattle, deer, and other species browse the twigs and eat the pods. A good honey plant. Native Americans made cakes and a fermented drink using flour made from the seeds. Commonly called mes-KEET but pronounced mes-keetay in Spanish.

VELVET MESQUITE *Prosopis velutina* Woot.

Much like Honey Mesquite but with 15-20 pairs of ± *hairy* minor leaflets each only ¼"-½" long and ¹⁄₁₆"-⅛" wide. Thorns often few. Spur branches *short*. Height to 50'. From cen. Arizona and sw. New Mexico south into Mexico.

SCREWBEAN MESQUITE *Prosopis pubescens* Benth.

A mesquite with unique, brown, *tightly-spiralled* fruit pods *1"-3"* long. Leaves only *1"-3"* in length with 5-9 pairs of minor leaflets ¼"-⅜" long and ⅛"-³⁄₁₆" wide. Seeds are eaten by bobwhite and Gambel quail, roadrunners, and other wildlife. Mainly s. California/s. Nevada/w. Arizona and the Rio Grande valley of New Mexico/Texas/Mexico; local in nearby areas.

In s. Arizona near the Mexican border: Huisache [*Acacia farnesiana* (L.) Willd.] has leaves with *4-8 pairs of major leaflets* and 10-25 pairs of minor leaflets each about ¼" long and ¹⁄₃₂" wide. Flower clusters are yellow, ball-shaped, and fragrant. Pronounced wee-SAH-chay. **Jerusalem-thorn** (*Parkinsonia aculeata* L.) has 40-60 minor leaflets per major leaflet. These drop early, leaving *2-6 grasslike midribs* each 8"-15" long as remnants of the major leaflets. Thorns often triple with one longer. Spur branches small. Also called Mexican Paloverde or Retama.

Plate 16

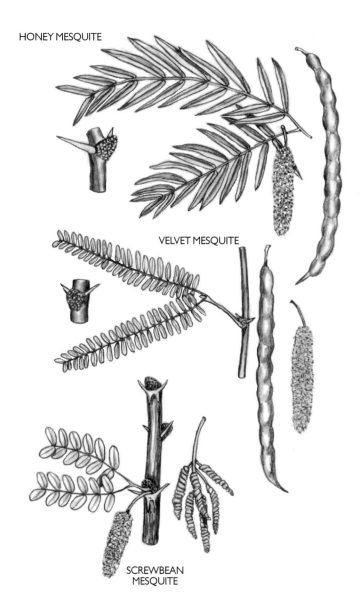

HONEY MESQUITE

VELVET MESQUITE

SCREWBEAN
MESQUITE

17. THORNS SINGLE, LEAVES TWICE-COMPOUND

Foliage divided into *major* leaflets and again into *minor* leaflets, the latter *blunt* and *not* toothed. Flowers *pealike*; fruits in *pods*. Arid and semi-arid sites in the Southwest. See Yellow Paloverde, Plate 21.

BLUE PALOVERDE *Cercidium floridum* A. Gray
A desert tree with leaves only ¾"-1" long, *mostly absent*. The ephemeral foliage has *one* pair of major leaflets, each with *1-3* pairs of minor leaflets only ³⁄₁₆"-¼" long and ± ¹⁄₁₆" wide. Unlike Yellow Paloverde (Plate 21), a *straight* thorn ¼"-⅜" in length occurs *at each node*. Thorns *straight*. Flowers showy, *yellow*, about ¾" wide, in loose clusters, March-May; fruit pods *flat*, 2"-3" long. Trunk and large branches mostly a *smooth blue-green*. Height to 30'. Young pods and seeds were foods of Native Americans. Desert washes and depressions from se. California and sw. Arizona into Mexico. Pah-low-VEHR-deh.

GREGG CATCLAW *Acacia greggii* A. Gray
An acacia with *hooked* thorns ¼"-⅜" long. Leaves *1"-3"* long with *1-3* pairs of major leaflets and *3-7* pairs of minor leaflets ⅛"-¼" long and ¹⁄₁₆" wide. Spur branches about ¼" long. Flowers *pale yellow*, in *slender* clusters, 2"-3" long, fragrant; fruit pods *much twisted*, brown, hairless. Trunk bark gray-brown, deeply fissured. Height 15'-30'. From sw. Utah, s. Nevada, and se. California across cen. and s. Arizona to w. Texas and nearby Mexico. Thicket-forming, drought-resistant; heavily browsed by deer and livestock despite the thorns. A fine honey plant. Native Americans once ate the fruit pods and ground the seeds into flour.

In w. Texas and adjoining Mexico there are three additional catclaws: **Roemer Catclaw** (*A. roemeriana* Scheele) is like Gregg Catclaw but leaves *2"-4"* long, minor leaflets ¼"-½" in length and ⅛"-¼" *wide*, thorns sometimes paired, and yellowish flower clusters *globular*. Also in se. New Mexico. **Wright Catclaw** (*A. wrightii* Benth.) has leaves *1"-3"* long, with only *1-2* pairs of major leaflets, and flowers in *slim spikes*. **Guajillo** (*A. berlandieri* Benth.) occasionally with thorns absent or not curved, has *large fernlike* leaves, the *5-12* pairs of major leaflets with numerous minor leaflets ⅛"-³⁄₁₆" long and ± ¹⁄₃₂" wide. **Also along the international border**, the planted ornamental and *straight-thorned* **Dwarf Poinciana** [*Caesalpinia pulcherrima* (L.) Sw.] may escape to the wild. Leaves are *nearly evergreen*, 5"-15" long, with *5-10* major and *6-10* minor leaflet pairs. Minor leaflets are ⅜"-¾" long and ± ⁵⁄₁₆" wide. Flowers large, *showy*, petals red and yellow, stamens long, red. "Dwarf" compared with Royal Poinciana or Flamboyant [*Delonix regia* (Bojer ex Hook.) Raf.], a large related flowering tree widely planted in the tropics.

Plate 17

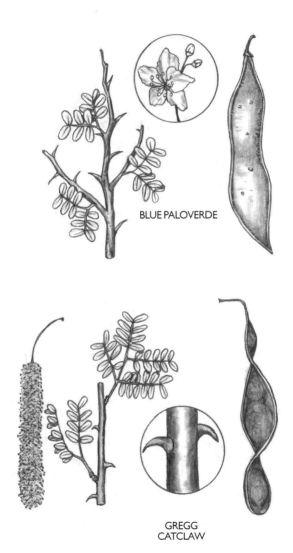

BLUE PALOVERDE

GREGG
CATCLAW

18. LEAVES ONCE-COMPOUND, TOOTHED
I: Walnuts and Tree-of-Heaven

These non-thorny trees haves *large* leaf scars that are either *shield-shaped or triangular*. Leaves are *10"-24"* long with 9-41 leaflets. Twigs and branchlets are *stout*; bundle scars are *many*. **Walnut** twigs show a *chambered* pith when cut lengthwise and leaves have a *spicy odor* when crushed. Male blossoms in slender catkins, spring; female flowers tiny. Fruits nearly *spherical*. Nut meat edible but difficult to extract; fruit husks will stain hands and clothes a penetrating brown (be careful!). Lumber is valuable for furniture. Bruised branches and foliage will stun fish, a practice illegal in the United States. English Walnut (*J. regia* L.), occasionally planted, has leaves not toothed. **Tree-of-Heaven** leaflets have *only 1-2 pairs* of gland-tipped teeth near the base.

ARIZONA WALNUT *Juglans major* (Torr.) A. Heller
Leaves 9"-13" long with *9-15* leaflets each 2"- 4" in length, ¾"-1¼" wide, long-pointed, *coarse-toothed*, and sometimes curved. Fruits *1"-1½"* in diameter. Height 30'-50'. Mountain valleys at 2000'-7500' elevation, south from cen. Arizona, w-cen. New Mexico, and cen. Texas to Mexico.

TEXAS WALNUT *Juglans microcarpa* Berlandier
A small-fruited walnut with leaves 8"-16" long and leaflets *15-21 (25)* in number, each 2"-6" long, only ¼"-½" wide, long-pointed, with or without *fine* teeth, and frequently curved. Fruits ¾"-1" in diameter. Height to 20'. Streamsides, sw. Kansas and nw. New Mexico south to Mexico.

TREE-OF-HEAVEN *Ailanthus altissima* (Mill.) Swingle
Chinese in origin and fast-growing, but generally of little value. Leaves *12"-24"* long with *11-41* leaflets each 2"-6" in length. Leaflets with *only 1-2 pairs of gland-teeth* near the leaf base. Twigs thick but weak, pith *continuous*; buds small, hairy. Flowers yellow, small, early summer; fruits one-seeded, papery, in large clusters, autumn. To 100' tall on disturbed sites throughout the United States. May grow 8' or more a year; sprouts 12' long are not unusual. The common name, probably of Asiatic origin, may allude to the tree's height.

Scientific names of Mexican-border trees listed on Plate 20:
Evergreen Sumac *Rhus choriophylla* Woots. & Standl., Mescalbean *Sophora secundiflora* (Ort.) Lag., Peru Peppertree *Schinus molle* L., Brazilian Peppertree *S. terebinthifolius* Raddi., Prairie Sumac *Rhus lanceolata* (Gray) Britton, Western Kidneywood *Eysenhardtia polystachya* (Ort.) Sarg., Elephant-tree *Bursera microphylla* Gray, Littleleaf Sumac *Rhus microphylla* Engelm., Littleleaf Lysiloma *Lysiloma microphylla* Benth., Goldenball Leadtree *Leucaena retusa* Benth., Paradise Poinciana *Caesalpinia gillesii* (Hook.) Dietr.

Plate 18

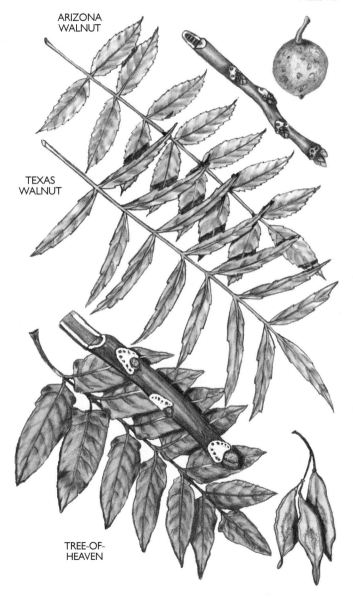

ARIZONA
WALNUT

TEXAS
WALNUT

TREE-OF-
HEAVEN

19. LEAVES ONCE-COMPOUND, TOOTHED
II: Mountain-ashes/Smooth Sumac

Though also with leaflets *toothed* (see Plate 18), the leaf scars here are *narrow*. **Mountain-ashes** have *crescentlike* leaf scars, bundle scars *3-5*, and spur branches *frequent*. Flower clusters are white and ± *flat-topped*; fruits are reddish, several-seeded, *applelike*, and ¼"-½" in diameter. Ruffed and sharptail grouse, ptarmigans, martens, and fishers eat the fruits, as do some people. Much used in landscaping. Some species grow as far north as Alaska, Labrador, Greenland, Iceland, and n. Europe. In Europe, often called rowan or servicetree, the latter possibly a corruption of Sorbustree and perhaps the basis for our serviceberry (Plate 37) name. **Smooth Sumac** is below. Common Hoptree (Plate 20) is occasionally fine-toothed.

SITKA MOUNTAIN-ASH *Sorbus sitchensis* Roem.
  The leaves of this small tree have 7-11 *blunt* or short-pointed leaflets with the basal ⅓-½ of the leaflet edges *not* toothed. Twigs and winter buds ± *rusty-hairy*. Flowers ± ¼" wide, the clusters *2"- 4"* in diameter, June-August; fruits *orange* to red, nearly ½" across, August-winter. Height to 20'. Sw. Alaska and sw. Yukon to cen. California. First found near Sitka, se. Alaska.

GREENE MOUNTAIN-ASH *Sorbus scopulina* E. Greene
  Often shrubby with leaflets *fully toothed*, *long-pointed*, and 11-15 per leaf. Twigs and buds *hairless*. Flowers ± ⅜" in diameter, in clusters *1"-3"* across, August-September; fruits *red*, ¼"-⅜" wide, July-August. Height to 20'. From sw. Alaska and s. Yukon to California and New Mexico. Botanist Edward L. Greene described the species. Also called Western Mountain-ash.

EUROPEAN MOUNTAIN-ASH *Sorbus aucuparia* L.
  Introduced into the East and now growing wild in scattered locations across the continent. Leaflets 9-15, *short-pointed*, *white-hairy* beneath, and toothed *nearly* to the base. Twigs/buds also *white-hairy*. Trunk with *horizontal streaks*. Flowers ⅜" wide, the clusters *4"- 6"* in diameter, May-June; fruits *red*, 5/16"-⅜" in diameter, August-October or later. Height to 40'. The species' name refers to the traditional use of the sticky sap to catch birds. Said to be the only exotic tree to grow wild in Alaska.

SMOOTH SUMAC *Rhus glabra* L.
  A small tree of the East with *11-31* long-pointed, *coarse-toothed* leaflets. Twigs stout, *flat-sided*; buds *white-hairy*; leaf scars *U-shaped*; bundle scars many, spur branches lacking. Flowers small, greenish, June-July; fruits tiny, dry, *red-hairy* clusters, July-winter. Height 4'-10' (25'). Local. Native Americans reportedly once ate the raw sprouts.

Mexican-buckeye (*Ungnadia speciosa* Endl.), found in se. New Mexico and Texas, has 5-7 coarse-toothed, long-pointed leaflets. The leaf scars and pear-shaped fruits are both 3-lobed.

Plate 19

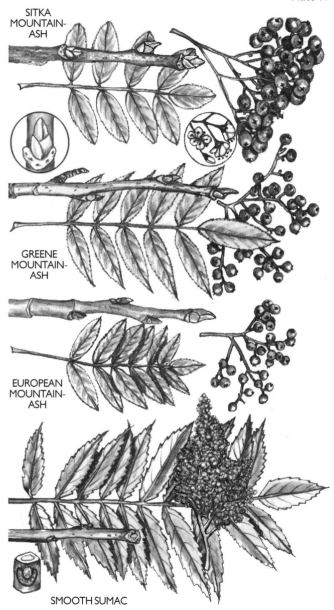

SITKA MOUNTAIN-ASH

GREENE MOUNTAIN-ASH

EUROPEAN MOUNTAIN-ASH

SMOOTH SUMAC

20. Mostly ONCE-COMPOUND, NOT TOOTHED

These southwestern trees have leaflets *not toothed*. The first two are the only ones likely to be encountered north of the Mexican border region. See also Texas Walnut and Tree-of-Heaven (Pl. 18).

COMMON HOPTREE *Ptelea trifoliata* L.

The only tree in the Rockies whose alternate foliage is deciduous and regularly *trifoliate*. Leaves are 4"-10" long with each of the three leaflets 1"-4" long and ½"-2" wide, *gland-dotted* (use lens), and occasionally fine-toothed. The end leaflet *short-stalked;* twigs hairless. Buds hairy, *hidden* beneath leafstalk bases in summer and nearly surrounded by *U-shaped* leaf scars in winter. Bundle scars three. Small, green, springtime blossoms produce *flat*, circular, *papery*, hoplike fruits ¾"-1" across. Trunk bark pale and smooth or shallowly grooved. Height to 15'. Ranging from s. Nevada, sw. Utah, and cen. Colorado into the eastern states. Foliage resembles Poison-oak [*Toxicodendron diversi-lobium* (Torrey & Gray) Greene] but the end leaflet of that irritating shrub is long-stalked.

WESTERN SOAPBERRY *Sapindus drummondii* Hook. & Arn.

A tree with leaves 4"-15" long and *8-18 narrow, long-pointed,* and somewhat-leathery but deciduous leaflets. Leaflets each 1"-3" long and ¾"-1" wide with the sides *unequal*. The end leaflet is often *lacking* but may be the only leaflet retained in winter. Buds small, hairy, and *partially imbedded* (use lens). Leaf scars triangular or 3-lobed and *not* surrounding the buds. There are three bundle scars. Flowers white, clustered, June-July; fruits fleshy, yellowish to white, *spherical*, ⅜"-½" in diameter, September-October or longer. Height 20'-50' (70'). Arizona/New Mexico east to the Mississippi Valley and south to Mexico.

Trees of the Mexican border region (see scientific names Plate 18): Of those with (1) once-compound *leathery* foliage, **Evergreen Sumac** has *2"-3"* leaves and 3-7 ± *pointed* leaflets, **Mescalbean Sophora** has *4"-6"* leaves and 5-9 *blunt* leaflets, **Peru Pepper-tree** has *17-41* slender leaflets, and **Brazilian Peppertree** has *red* midribs. Those with (2) once-compound *deciduous* leafage include **Prairie Sumac** with 11-23 *pointed* leaflets 1"-3" long, and several trees with *blunt* leaflets *under* ¾" long: **Western Kidneywood** (se. Arizona, *20-56* leaflets per leaf), **Elephant-tree** (sw. Arizona, *20-40* such leaflets), and **Littleleaf Sumac** (with only *5-9* mostly-blunt leaflets). Trees with (3) *twice-compound evergreen* leafage are **Littleleaf Lysiloma** of se. Arizona with minor leaflets only ¹⁄₁₆" *wide*, **Goldenball Leadtree** of w. Texas with minor leaflets ± ½" wide, and **Paradise Poinciana**, a garden escape like the Peppertrees, with *hairy* twigs and leaflets ¹⁄₁₆"-⅛" wide. See also Guajillo (Plate 17), sometimes thornless.

Plate 20

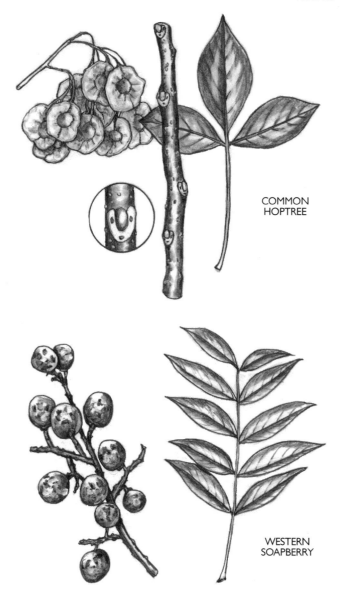

COMMON
HOPTREE

WESTERN
SOAPBERRY

V. Trees with Alternate Simple Leaves

Nearly half of Rocky Mountains trees have broadleaf foliage of this type. Thin *deciduous* leaves occur on 66 species while 27 kinds have mostly leathery, *evergreen* leafage. But see Yellow Paloverde below.

21. LEAFLESS DESERT TREES, TWIGS SPINE-TIPPED

Leaves are *much reduced in size* (to ¼"-1") and *present for only a short time* in spring. The *mostly-greenish* twigs and branches function as foliage in the photosynthetic process. Flowers are in lateral clusters. First three species all sometimes called Crucifixion-thorn. Only Canotia reaches north to s. Utah. Desert Apricot and Bitter Condalia (Plate 22) also often are leafless.

ALLTHORN *Koeberlinia spinosa* Zucc.

An extremely-thorny species with *stout*, yellow- or blue-green twigs 1"- 2" long, mostly at *right angles* to the branchlets, and with short, *black* spiny ends. Flowers greenish, in small clusters, March-July; fruits shiny, *black berries* ¼" wide. Ranges from se. California, cen. Arizona, cen. New Mexico, and s. Texas to cen. Mexico. Jackrabbits browse the twigs; scaled quail eat the fruits. C. L. Koeberlin was a 19th century German botanist.

CRUCIFIXION-THORN *Castela emoryi* (Gray) Moran & Felger

This small tree has stiff, *stout*, yellow-green twigs mostly 3"-5" long and ± fine-hairy (use lens). The tiny leaf scars are *greenish-white* (use lens). Flowers purplish, about ¼" across, densely clustered, June-July. Brown, dry, 1-seeded fruits *persist* on the tree *in starlike rings*. Height to 15'. Desert washes, se. California and sw. Arizona to nw. Mexico. Lt. Col. William Emory directed the Mexican boundary survey. Formerly *Holacantha.*

CANOTIA *Canotia holacantha* Torr.

The *slim*, yellow-green, fine-grooved (use lens) twigs of this species show tiny, *black*, and ± triangular leaf scars (use lens). Flowers greenish, in small groups, May-August; fruits dry, persistent, 5- (10-) parted capsules, ½" long. Older trunk bark *dark*. To 20' tall. Deserts, s. Utah and Arizona to nw. Mexico.

SMOKETHORN *Psorothamnus spinosa* (A. Gray) Barnaby

Gray-green, white-hairy, and *slender* twigs give a *smoky* tinge to this plant. Leaf scars are brownish (use lens). Flowers purple, June; fruits tiny, 1-seeded pea-pods. Trunk *gray*. Height to 25'. Se. California, s. Nevada, and sw. Arizona. Formerly *Dalea.*

YELLOW PALOVERDE *Cercidium microphyllum* (Torr.) Rose & Johnst.

(A compound-leaved tree but usually leafless, therefore reviewed here.) Common along desert washes of se. California, s. Arizona, and nw. Mexico, usually with a smooth *yellow-green* trunk and branches. Springtime leaves ¾"-1" long with two major leaflets each with 4-8 pairs of minor leaflets. The *slender* twigs have small *dark* leaf scars. Compare Blue Paloverde, Plate 17.

Plate 21

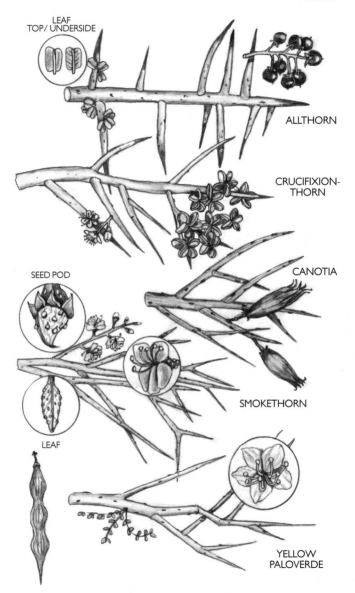

LEAF
TOP/ UNDERSIDE

ALLTHORN

CRUCIFIXION-
THORN

CANOTIA

SEED POD

LEAF

SMOKETHORN

YELLOW
PALOVERDE

22. THORNY TREES with LEAVES NORMAL

In our area, only these few trees with alternate simple foliage regularly produce woody thorns or sharp-tipped spur branches. They mostly have three bundle scars and white springtime flowers. All except the last two southwestern species have leaves toothed; Hollyleaf Buckthorn is evergreen. Russian-olive (Plate 33), with silvery foliage, sometimes bears woody thorns. Prickly-leaved plants, such as some oaks (Plate 27), are not classed as thorny.

Hawthorns are shrubs or small trees with dense foliage. Thorns *slender*, 1"-2" long, occurring on *both* twigs and older wood, and mostly *not* bearing buds or leaves. Leaf bases *V-shaped*; spur branches mostly *absent*. Fruits small, applelike, mostly *several-seeded*, summer-winter. Though easily identified as a group, even experts have difficulty in recognizing species. Black Hawthorn is the most common in the West and serves here as an example of the genus. Hawthorns are favored by songbirds as nest sites. May invade pastures. Most species shrubby. Some used in landscaping.

BLACK HAWTHORN *Crataegus douglasii* Lindl.
Foliage 1"-4" long, *coarsely double-toothed* or irregularly shallow-lobed, and mostly *hairless*. Thorns *⅓"-1"* long. Mature fruits *black*. Height to 25'. From cen. British Columbia to cen. Arizona/New Mexico. Also called Thornapple.

AMERICAN PLUM *Prunus americana* Marsh.
A small tree or shrub of the northern plains ranging eastward from w. Montana, cen. Colorado, and cen. New Mexico. Leaves 1"-5" long, about half as wide, ± long-pointed, sharply and mostly *double-toothed*. Leafstalk glands *lacking*. Thorns mostly short, stiff, bud-bearing spur branches; twigs sometimes hairy. Fruits red or yellow, ¾"-1" in diameter, *single-seeded*. Height 15'-30'. Thicket-forming. Fruits much eaten by wildlife.

Trees of the Southwest with thorn-tipped twigs:

Desert Apricot (*Prunus fremontii* Wats.), with *nearly circular* leaves mostly under 1" long, occurs southward from se. California. **Hollyleaf Buckthorn** (*Rhamnus ilicifolia* Kellogg), a shrub or small tree with *evergreen*, leathery, *prickly-edged* leaves only ¼"-1" long and with parallel veins , grows to 25' in height over much of California/Arizona. **Bitter Condalia** (*Condalia globosa* Johnst.) is an *extremely-spiny* tree of desert mountains in se. California, sw. Arizona, and nw. Mexico. It has *smooth-edged*, blunt, wedge-based leaves ¼"-½" long and twigs that grow *at right angles* to each other. **Gum Bumelia** [*Bumelia lanuginosa* (Michx.) Pers.] with leaves blunt-tipped, V-based, ± leathery, and 1"-4" long occurs in se. Arizona/sw. New Mexico and southward. Sap *milky*.

Plate 22

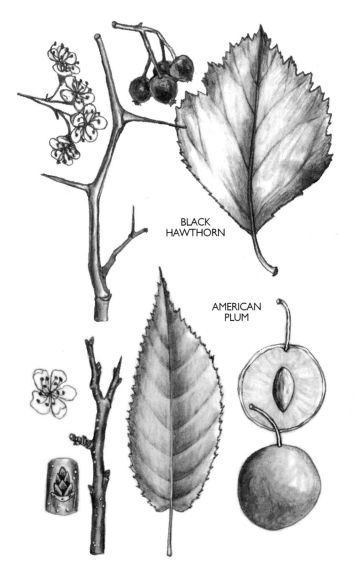

BLACK
HAWTHORN

AMERICAN
PLUM

23. THORNLESS TREES: LEAVES FAN-LOBED

Of these trees, the last three may have both fan-lobed and fan-veined leaves (see also White Poplar, Plate 25). Some hawthorns (Plate 22) also may have lobed leaves but the trees are thorny.

ARIZONA SYCAMORE *Platanus wrightii* S.Wats.

Sycamores typically are floodplain trees with *mottled* and *flaky* outer brown bark exposing a *pale* underbark, but in this species the trunk and main branches may be nearly white. Leaves deeply 5-7 lobed, 4"-10" long, and *without* teeth. Leafstalk with a *hollow* base that covers the bud. A leaf scar with *many* bundle scars *surrounds* each bud. Bud with a *single* caplike scale. A leafy stipule *encircles* the twig near each bud, leaving a stipule scar that *rings* the winter twig. Springtime heads of small, fuzzy, greenish flowers produce tiny, hairy, brown fruits held tightly in inch-wide *balls*. 3-5 balls hang on each stalk. Height to 80'. Elevations of 2000'-5000' from cen. Arizona and sw. New Mexico to nw. Mexico. Willows (Plates 29-32), also show a single bud scale but otherwise are quite different.

CALIFORNIA FREMONTIA *Fremontodendron californicum* (Torr.) Cov.

Our only regional shrub or small tree with *evergreen* fan-lobed foliage. A brightly-flowered plant with leaves leathery, mostly only *1"-2"* long, rather *sandpapery* above, *densely hairy* beneath, and long-stalked. Usually 3-5 lobes per leaf with 1-3 main veins meeting at the leafbase. Some leaves *wavy-toothed*, others smooth-edged. Twigs and buds *brown-hairy*; buds *without* scales; bundle scar *single*; spur branches present. Blossoms *yellow*, showy, 1"-2½" wide, May-June; fruit capsules hairy, egg-shaped, 1"-1¼" long, August-September. Sometimes to 25' tall. Named after John C. Frémont, 19th century frontiersman. Foothills to 6000' elevation, n. California and cen. Arizona to Baja California.

TEXAS MULBERRY *Morus microphylla* Buckl.

A small-leaved mulberry with toothed *deciduous* leaves *rough-hairy* on both sides, only *1"-3"* long, and either deeply fan-lobed or merely fan-veined. Twigs ± hairless, bud with 3-5 red-brown scales, bundle scars 4 or more, and sap *milky* in warm weather. Flowers inconspicuous, March-April; fruits *blackberrylike*, edible, May-June. Height to 20'. From cen. and s. Arizona east to s. Oklahoma and s. Texas. Also n. Mexico. Inner bark *fibrous*, can be twisted into cords and pounded into bark cloth.

WHITE MULBERRY *Morus alba* L.

Like the last species but leaves *3"-10"* long, mostly 3-5-lobed, *hairless*. Bud scales 5-6. Fruits *whitish*, ± tasteless. Introduced from China in 1600s to raise silkworms. Widely naturalized.

Plate 23

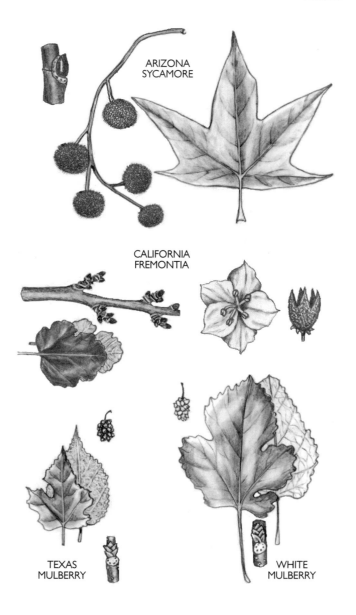

ARIZONA
SYCAMORE

CALIFORNIA
FREMONTIA

TEXAS
MULBERRY

WHITE
MULBERRY

24. LEAVES FAN-VEINED OR HEART-SHAPED

These mostly-southwestern trees have deciduous leaves that regularly have three or more main veins meeting at the leaf base. Some plants of Plate 23 and most poplars (Plate 25) also may show such venation. Unlike the species of Plate 23, these trees have *three* bundle scars . **Hackberries** have foliage mostly *long-pointed*, leaf bases mainly *uneven*, and pith *chambered* (solid at least at the leaf nodes). Twigs smooth, round. Flowers inconspicuous, fruits small, brown, *one-seeded* spheres with a thin, somewhat sweet-tasting covering. **Redbuds** have leaves deeply *heart-shaped* to nearly round, and leaf edges smooth. Twigs are hairless, vigorous twigs often showing 1-3 lines descending from the leaf scars. Pith *continuous*. Fruits flat, brown *pods*.

NETLEAF HACKBERRY *Celtis reticulata* Torr.

Widespread in the American West with the dark trunk rather smooth but marked by prominent *warty knobs*. Leaves only *1"-3"* long, *thick*, often *sandpapery* above, *net-veined* beneath, and with *few* teeth or none. Height to 50'. Dry slopes and streamsides, ranging from n-cen. Washington and n. Idaho to s. California, n. Mexico, s-cen. Texas, and the s. Great Plains. Often called Western Hackberry or Sugarberry.

NORTHERN HACKBERRY *C. occidentalis* L.

An eastern species that ranges west to e. Wyoming and ne. Colorado with foliage *3"-6"* in length, *thin*, sandpapery, and *sharp-toothed to below the middle*. Native Americans reportedly boiled the bark as treatment for sore throat.

SOUTHERN HACKBERRY *C. laevigata* Willd.

Extending its eastern range to w. Texas, this tree has leaves *2"-6"* long, ± *leathery*, *smooth-surfaced*, and teeth few or *none*.

CALIFORNIA REDBUD *Cercis occidentalis* Torr.

Leaves 2"-5" long, somewhat leathery, and *nearly round*. Before the springtime leaves appear, short-stemmed, red-purple, half-inch blossoms outline the branchlets and provide *showy* springtime displays. Flowers, not buds, are reddish. Mature fruits are 2"-3" long and *⅝"-¾"* wide, July-August. Local, s. Utah, n. and cen. Arizona. Flowers reported sometimes to be eaten in salads. Dried red branch wood is used in basketry; the roots yield a red dye.

EASTERN REDBUD *Cercis canadensis* L.

An eastern tree that reaches w. Texas and se. New Mexico as var. *texensis* (Wats.) Hopkins. Much like California Redbud, but the leaves are *short-pointed* and fruit pods are *under ½"* in width.

Plate 24

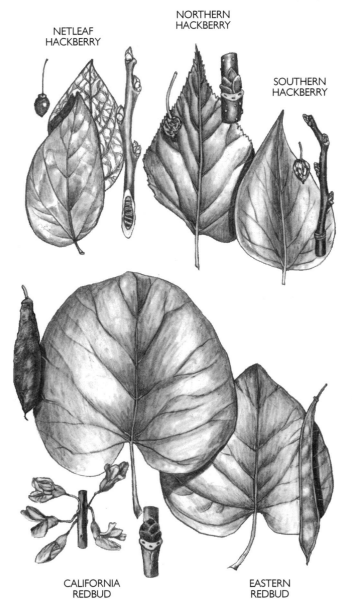

NETLEAF
HACKBERRY

NORTHERN
HACKBERRY

SOUTHERN
HACKBERRY

CALIFORNIA
REDBUD

EASTERN
REDBUD

25. POPLARS: Aspen, Cottonwoods

The common names vary but all are related poplars. Leaves are broadly rounded or triangular, long-stalked, and often with 3-5 main veins meeting at the base (but see Narrowleaf Cottonwood). The lowermost bud scale is *directly above the leaf scar*; flowers and fruits are in catkins. Trunks are often smooth and whitish when young. Several species have *flattened* leafstalks.

QUAKING ASPEN *Populus tremuloides* Michx.

Leaves 2"-6" long with *nearly circular* and *fine-toothed* blades that become golden in autumn. Leafstalks *flattened*, enabling foliage to flutter in a breeze. Twigs *dark brown* with the end bud *smooth* and only ¼"-⅜" long. Young bark *chalk-white to greenish*. Height to 75'. Distributed from n. Alaska to Mexico. This tree spreads mostly by root sprouts and estimates are that some groves have survived for 10,000 years (see Plate 3).

FREMONT COTTONWOOD *Populus fremontii* S.Wats.

Ranging south from nw. Colorado and cen. Nevada, this is a tree of the Southwest. Leaves are *coarse-toothed*, mostly *triangular*, 2"-5" long, and generally with a tapered tip. Leafstalks *flattened*. Twigs *yellowish*, with the end bud smooth and ⅜"-½" long. Mature trunk dark with deep grooves. Moist sites. To 100' tall. John C. Frémont, was a 19th century explorer and politician.

BLACK COTTONWOOD

Populus balsamifera var. *trichocarpa* (Torr. & Gray) Brayshaw

Leaves 4"-8" long, triangular, *fine-toothed*, dark green above, mostly *silver-white* beneath, leafbase glands frequent. Leafstalks *not* flat. Twigs brownish; end bud ¾"-⅞" long, *gummy*, and *aromatic* when crushed. Fruit capsules ± hairless, 3-parted. Height to 165'. Floodplains, from sw. Alaska to nw. Mexico and inland to e-cen. British Columbia, sw. Alberta, s-cen. Montana, n. Utah, and the Sierra Nevada. Wood used for paper pulp, boxes, and rough lumber. Now made a subspecies of **Balsam Poplar** (*P. balsamifera* L.) which ranges east across Canada and n. U.S. from most of Alaska and Yukon to cen. Colorado with leaves only pale beneath and fruit capsules ± hairy, 2-parted. **Eastern Cottonwood** (*P. deltoides* Bartr.) extends east from sw. Alberta, ne. Utah, and ne.Arizona with wide, *heart-shaped* leaves, *glands* at the leaf base, and *stalks flattened*.

NARROWLEAF COTTONWOOD *Populus angustifolia* James

Mainly a Rocky Mountains species, ranging from sw. Alberta to n. Mexico. Leaves *willowlike*, 3"-5" long, 1"-2" wide, *fine-toothed*; twigs yellowish; buds *sticky*. Height to 60'. Damp sites.

Naturalized European species: White Poplar (*P. alba* L.) has 2"-6" leaves triangular or lobed like maples. Foliage, twigs, and buds are *white-woolly*. **Lombardy Poplar** (*P. nigra* var. *italica* Muenchh.),tall, thin, and *columnar*, is often planted for ornament.

Plate 25

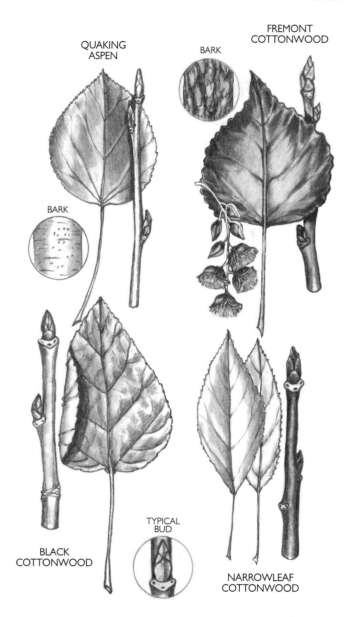

QUAKING
ASPEN

BARK

FREMONT
COTTONWOOD

BARK

BLACK
COTTONWOOD

TYPICAL
BUD

NARROWLEAF
COTTONWOOD

26. END BUDS CLUSTERED plus ACORNS: Oaks I

Regardless of foliage, oaks (Plates 26-28) are our only trees with *end buds clustered* at the twig tips and *more than three* bundle scars per leaf scar. Oaks also, of course, bear *acorn* fruits. In late spring, male blossoms occur in slender, *drooping* catkins several inches long while female flowers are small and unobtrusive. Acorns, green at first, become brown when mature. They are held in basal *cups* that, nevertheless, are commonly described as either bowl-shaped or saucerlike. Jumping-bean Sapium (Plate 33), Fire Cherry (Plate 36), and Cascara Buckthorn (Plate 37) also may have buds clustered at or near the twig ends but other field marks are evident.

An oak species is often classified as a member of either the white or red oak group. The lobe and leaf tips of white oaks *lack* the protruding hairlike *bristles* that are present in red oaks. Also, the acorns of white oaks require only one year to mature while those of red oaks take two. Thus, white oak acorns grow *only* on twigs while red oaks may have developing acorns on twigs *as well as* on branchlets. In addition, the inner surface of the shells (not cups) of white oaks are *hairless* while those of red oak acorns are ± *hairy*. Still further, the acorn meat of white oaks is light-colored and more edible in contrast to that of red oaks which usually contains much dark tannic acid and is bitter. Canyon Live Oak (Plate 27), an exception to some of these guidelines, is one of several species called intermediate oaks.

The trees of this plate are mostly white oaks with somewhat leathery yet *deciduous* foliage, the edges either *lobed* or *toothed*:

GAMBEL OAK *Quercus gambelii* Nutt.
> The only oak in the cen. and s. Rockies with deeply-lobed foliage. Leaves 2"-6" long. From n. Utah and s. Wyoming south to Mexico. Height to 65'. William Gambel collected Rocky Mountains plants in 1844.

WAVYLEAF OAK Often regarded as *Quercus undulata* Torr.
> An apparent complex of hybrids between Gambel Oak and either Havard, Chinkapin, Turbinella, Gray, Arizona, or Mohr oaks. Leaves 1"-3" long and variable, with deep lobes or large teeth.

Barely reaching our area: **Havard (Shin) Oak** (*Q. havardii* Rydb.) ranges from nw. Oklahoma to se. New Mexico (also se. Utah), the leaves 2"-4" long, shallow-lobed, wavy-edged, or neither. **Chinkapin Oak** (*Q. muhlenbergii* Engelm.), an eastern tree, occurs also in se. New Mexico and w. Texas with *thin* leaves sharply toothed. **Graves Oak** (*Q. gravesii* Sudw.), a *red* oak of w. Texas and ne. Mexico has non-leathery leaves with deep bristle-tipped lobes. **Bur (Mossycup) Oak** (*Q. macrocarpa* Michx.) has fringed acorn cup scales and deeply lobed leaves divided by a narrow "waist" into two uneven major parts. It ranges west to se. Montana and ne. Wyoming.

Plate 26

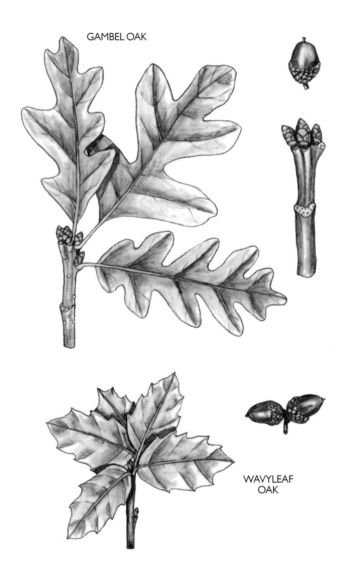

GAMBEL OAK

WAVYLEAF OAK

27. END BUDS CLUSTERED plus ACORNS: Oaks II

Oaks are mostly valuable timber trees and bear acorns that are essential in the diets of deer, squirrels, and many other wildlife species. Acorns also once served as important foods for Native Americans. Even the bitter acorns of red oaks were rendered edible by grinding the kernels and treating the flour with hot water. Reportedly, early settlers used dried acorn shells as a coffee substitute. In Spanish, roble (ROHB-leh) is the general name for a deciduous oak species; encino (en-SEEN-oh) is used for an evergreen oak.

Leaves of oaks on this plate are mostly only ½"-2½" long, leathery, *evergreen, prickly-edged* and hollylike. Twigs are usually hairy (use lens) and acorn cups mostly bowl-shaped. The *crinkled* edges of Sandpaper Oak may be described as curled, crisped, or up-and-down wavy. The first two species are members of the white oak group (see Plate 26). Canyon Live Oak is an intermediate oak.

Hollyleaf Buckthorn (Plate 22), Wavyleaf Oak (Plate 26), and oaks of Plate 28 have leaves sometimes prickly and often longer.

SANDPAPER OAK *Quercus pungens* Liebm.
Usually shrubby but occasionally becoming 25' tall. Foliage ¾"-2" long, *crinkled*, light- to *dark-green*, with *rough-hairy* (sandpapery) surfaces, and *V-shaped* bases. Occasionally lobed or without teeth. Acorns narrowly cylindrical, the cups on ¹⁄₁₆"-⅛" stalks. Rocky slopes, se. Arizona, cen. New Mexico, and cen. Texas south to Mexico. The specific name means sharp, prickly. Scrub Oak is another name for this and some other oaks.

TURBINELLA OAK *Quercus turbinella* Greene
Foliage is *flat*, 1"-2" long, dull *gray-green*, *hairless above*, usually fine-hairy beneath, the leaf bases ± *U-shaped*, and edges sometimes only slightly wavy. Distributed from California, s. Nevada, s. Utah, and s-cen. Colorado to Arizona and New Mexico.

CANYON LIVE OAK *Quercus chrysolepis* Liebm.
Leaves *1"-2½"* long, *flat*, often whitened or *yellowish* beneath, and somewhat *waxy*. Side veins are mostly *parallel*. Acorn cups deep, thick-walled, and often *gold-hairy*. Called an intermediate oak because, like a red oak, the fruits require two years to mature and have hairy inner acorn shells (not cups). They grow on wood, however, that does not normally produce new growth during the second year and thus *appear* to mature on twigs like white oaks. To 60' tall. Mainly in California, local in cen. and se. Arizona. The dense wood once was made into wedges and mauls (heavy hammers) to split logs. Also called Maul Oak. The term live oak refers to the *evergreen* foliage (see Plate 28).

Plate 27

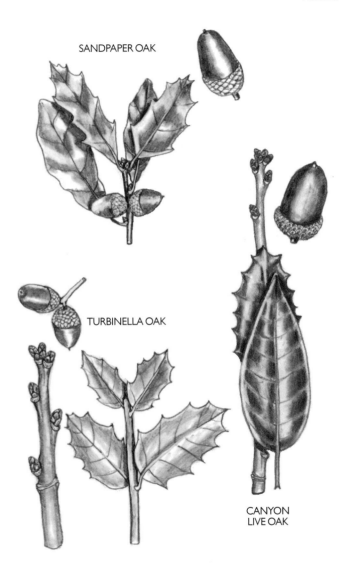

SANDPAPER OAK

TURBINELLA OAK

CANYON
LIVE OAK

28. END BUDS CLUSTERED plus ACORNS: Oaks III

Like all oaks, those of this plate have leaves and buds clustered at
the twig tips and produce acorns. Called live oaks because of their
evergreen foliage, these species have leaves thick, rather leathery,
and either toothed or not. They are *seldom* prickly-edged and most
have longer leaves than the trees of Plate 27. The first two species
have dull leaf surfaces; the others have mostly shiny foliage. A few
species have leaf undersides with veins prominently raised. Acorn
cups are mostly bowl-shaped and short-stalked. All are white oaks
(see Plate 26) except Emory, Silverleaf, Chisos, and Lateleaf oaks.

GRAY OAK *Quercus grisea* Liebm.

> An oak with *dull-surfaced* leaves *1"-3"* long, tips *pointed*, bases
> U- or heart-shaped, and teeth few or none. Height to 65'. Rocky
> slopes and canyons, n-cen. Arizona/w. Texas to cen. Mexico.

ARIZONA OAK *Quercus arizonica* Sarg.

> Also with *dull* foliage but leaves *1"-4"* in length, mostly *blunt*,
> *widest near the tip*, with *veins prominent* beneath. Acorn stalks
> short but sometimes to ¾". Height to 65'. Rocky slopes,
> cen. Arizona/cen. New Mexico/w. Texas to cen. Mexico.
> Sometimes regarded as a part of *Q. grisea.*

EMORY OAK *Quercus emoryi* Torr.

> Leaves 1"-3" (4") long, hairless, *narrow*, *pointed*, and *shiny
> green on both sides.* An intermediate oak with hairy inner acorn
> shells (not cups) and nuts that mature in one year on twiglike
> branchlets. Height to 80". Cen. Arizona to w. Texas. William
> Emory explored the Mexican border region in early 1800s.

MOHR OAK *Quercus mohriana* Buckl.

> Thicket-forming, from ne. New Mexico and cen. Oklahoma
> south to w. and cen. Texas and n. Mexico. Foliage *egg-shaped*,
> 1"-4" long, *white-hairy beneath*, the edges *not* rolled under. Low
> hills and plains. Charles Mohr was a naturalist of the late 1800s.

Near the Mexican border: Silverleaf Oak (*Q. hypoleucoides*
A. Camus) has narrow, pointed leaves 1"-4" long, dark green above,
silver-hairy and veiny beneath, teeth few or none, the edges *rolled under*.
Netleaf Oak (*Q. rugosa* Née) leaves are mostly convex, prominently
veined on both sides, and often toothed toward the tip. Acorn cups are on
1"-3" stalks. **Toumey Oak** (*Q. toumeyi* Sarg.) foliage is only ½"-1½"
in length with pointed tips and often many teeth. **Mexican Blue Oak**
(*Q. oblongifolia* Torr.) has unique blue-gray, parallel-sided, blunt leaves
only 1"-4" long, with no teeth. Except Toumey and Mexican Blue oaks,
the above species range east to w. Texas. In w. Texas, little-known **Chisos
Oak** (*Q. gracilifornis* C. H. Muller) and **Lateleaf Oak** (*Q. tardifolia* C.
H. Muller) are bristle-tipped red oaks, the former with coppery, drooping
foliage and the latter with leaves green and shallow-lobed.

Plate 28

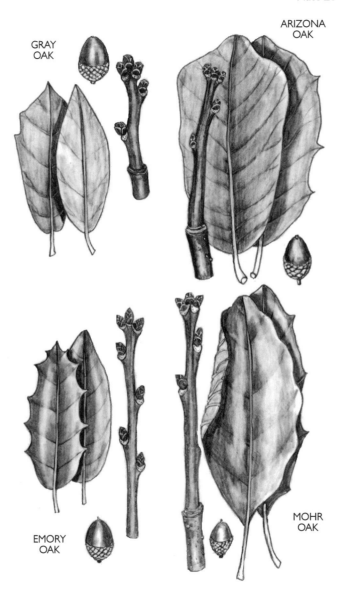

GRAY
OAK

ARIZONA
OAK

EMORY
OAK

MOHR
OAK

29. BUDS WITH ONE SCALE: Willows I

Many willows, but not all, can be recognized by their slender leaves. All willows, however, have buds with *only one scale*, the scale edges mostly fused (overlapping in only four species). Leaves of most species are whitened beneath, upper ends of leafstalks are mostly *without* glands, stipules are usually *small* or absent. Twigs are mostly hairless, bundle scars are *three*, the end bud is false. Flowers and fruits (which experts must examine microscopically for the certain identification of some species) are arranged in slender, caterpillarlike *catkins*. Trunks dark and rough.

Vegetative characters are variable and hybrids are common. Willows tend to grow on moist sites; many are shrubby. Arizona Sycamore (Plate 23), also with a single bud scale, is otherwise different. See Narrowleaf Cottonwood (Plate 25).

The trees of this plate have leaves *very narrow* (8-15 times longer than wide) and mostly 2"-6" long. (See also Bonpland Willow, Plate 31). Most species have gray-green foliage. Except as noted, the leaf edges are *fine-toothed*.

Willow twigs are eaten by deer, elk, moose, caribou, rabbits, hares, and many rodents. Salicin, a chemical derived from willow bark, is the original substance from which aspirin was developed.

SANDBAR WILLOW *Salix exigua* Nutt.
A streamside species with *very* narrow, *parallel-sided*, short-or *long-pointed* leaves only ⅛"-½" wide. Leaf undersides and twigs often *white-hairy*. Leaf teeth wide, often *few*, rarely none; stalks ±⅛" long. Buds to ¼". To 20' tall. Nearly transcontinental, south from cen. Alaska. The long twigs/branchlets may be woven into baskets.

GOODDING WILLOW *Salix gooddingii* C. Ball
Leaves fine-toothed, *hairless*, short-pointed, and *green* beneath. Leafstalks ± ¼" long with glands *present* at or near the leaf base. Twigs *yellowish* and ± hairy; buds to ⅛". The edges of the single bud scale are *not fused* but show as a line on the smooth bud (use lens). Southwestern states and nearby Mexico.

YEWLEAF WILLOW *Salix taxifolia* H.B.H.
A desert tree with gray-hairy leaves only ½"-1¾" long, ⅛"-³⁄₁₆" wide, and short-pointed. Twigs hairy, often drooping. Height to 40'. Se. Arizona and w. Texas south to Guatemala.

Weeping Willow (*Salix babylonica* L.), often planted, is an Old World tree with *extremely* long twigs and branchlets that *hang vertically*. Leaves *long-pointed*, white-hairy beneath, with teeth few or none, and edges turned under. Leafstalks to ¼", *glands* present. Buds to ⅛" in length. Height to 50'.

Plate 29

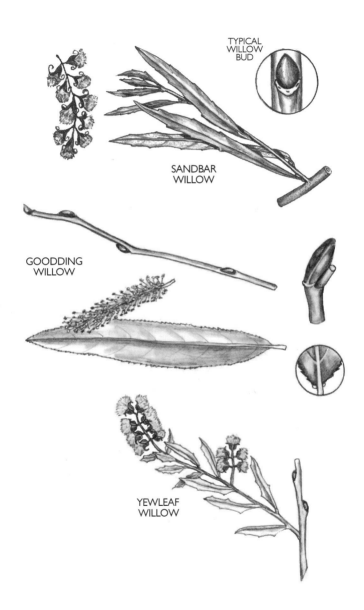

TYPICAL WILLOW BUD

SANDBAR WILLOW

GOODDING WILLOW

YEWLEAF WILLOW

30. BUDS WITH ONE SCALE: Willows II

The willows of this plate have leaves mostly *without* teeth and with *V-shaped* leaf bases. The first two species have leaves of medium width (length is 5-7 times width); the last three have wider foliage (2-4 times longer than broad). Leaves of Bebb Willow (Plate 32) also sometimes lack teeth. For willows in general, see Plate 29.

GEYER WILLOW *Salix geyeriana* Anderss.

Leaves ± blunt, silky-hairy, only *1"-3"* long, ⅜"-½" wide, and ± whitened beneath. Twigs ± reddish, often with a whitish powder; buds *less than ⅛"* long. Height to 15'. At 5000'-7000' from s. British Columbia to ne. Utah and cen. Colorado. Also the Sierra Nevada, w-cen. Nevada, and cen. Arizona. Karl Geyer, a German botanist, collected western plants in the 1840s.

ARROYO WILLOW *Salix lasiolepis* Benth.

Leaves short-pointed or blunt, *shiny*, whitish beneath, rather *leathery*, ± *thickened*, 2"-5" long, and ½"-1" wide. Twigs ± hairless, yellowish; buds *over ¼"* long. Height to 30'. Mainly below 7000'. Widespread in the coast ranges; local inland from n-cen. Washington to n-cen. New Mexico and nw. Mexico.

FELTLEAF WILLOW *Salix alaxensis* (Anderss.) Cov.

A *broad-leaved* willow with foliage (and usually twigs) *densely white-woolly*. Leaves 2"-4" long, ½"-1½" wide, yellow-green, bases V-shaped, stipules small and slim. The most northern of tree willows, ranging across most of mainland Alaska, n. British Columbia, and Yukon. Absent from the lower 48 states.

SCOULER WILLOW *Salix scouleriana* Hook

Leaves mostly blunt, *2"-5"* long, ½"-1½" wide, *shiny*, and ± wavy-edged. Foliage *widest toward the tip*, whitish and often somewhat hairy beneath. Twigs yellowish to dark and usually *drooping*; buds *over ¼"* long. Height to 25'. Throughout the Rocky Mountains at elevations below 7000' from s. Alaska to Mexico. John Scouler, a Scottish physician, studied plants along the Pacific Coast in the early 19th century.

SITKA WILLOW *Salix sitchensis* Bong.

A willow with leaves *dull* above, densely *shiny-velvety* beneath, *short-pointed*, widest *above the middle*, mostly without teeth, and the edges strongly *rolled under*. Foliage *2"-4"* long, ¾"-1½" wide, and short-pointed or blunt. Twigs mostly *white-hairy*. Coastal from s. Alaska to n. California as well as inland across s. British Columbia. In the Rockies, from ne. British Columbia to e. Oregon and sw. Alberta.

Plate 30

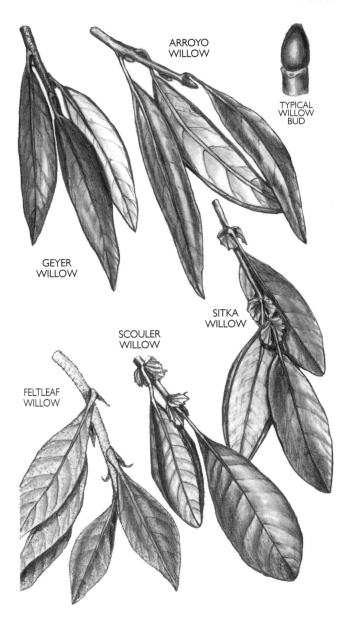

ARROYO
WILLOW

TYPICAL
WILLOW
BUD

GEYER
WILLOW

SITKA
WILLOW

SCOULER
WILLOW

FELTLEAF
WILLOW

31. BUDS WITH ONE SCALE: Willows III

These species have leaves mostly of *medium width* (5-7 times longer than wide). Leaves mostly *fine-toothed*, *hairless*, *whitened* beneath, and *long-pointed*. Bases mainly *U-shaped*, stalks generally *without* glands (use lens). Twigs usually hairless and winter buds mostly *under ⅛"* long. Heights 20'-80'. In the last three species of this page, the edges of the single bud scale are *not fused* but show as a line on the smooth bud (use lens, see also Goodding Willow, Plate 29). Crack and White willows, European imports, are listed on Plate 32. Littletree Willow (Plate 32) foliage is sometimes of medium width. Narrowleaf Cottonwood (Plate 25) is quite willowlike.

PACIFIC WILLOW *Salix lucida* ssp. *lasiandra* (Benth.) E.Murray
Leaves 2"-5" long, ½"-1" wide, shiny, dark green above, stipules common. Leafstalks ½"-¾" long with *glands present*. Buds *over ¼"* in length. In the Rockies from cen. Alaska and cen. Yukon to Arizona and New Mexico. Formerly *Salix lasiandra* Benth. Useful for making charcoal.

MACKENZIE WILLOW *Salix prolixa* Anderss.
Leaves *short-pointed*, dark green above, the bases U- or ± *heart-shaped*. Leaves 2½"-4" long, ⅝"-1½" wide, stipules frequent. Leafstalks ¼"-¾" in length. Twigs *red-brown* to yellowish, sometimes hairy. Found from se. Yukon and ne. Alberta to cen. California and nw. Wyoming. Also named *S. mackenzieana* or regarded as a variety of *S. rigida*.

MEADOW WILLOW *Salix petiolaris* J. E. Smith
Leaves 2"-4" long, ⅜"-¾" wide, shiny, dark green above, *V-based*, with stalks ¼"-½" in length. Young leaves usually *turn black* upon drying. Twigs tend to be clustered near the branchlet ends. Buds ⅛"-¼" long. In the Rockies, local from ne. British Columbia, sw. Alberta, to cen. Colorado.

BONPLAND WILLOW *Salix bonplandiana* Kunth.
Leaves ± *thick*, firm, 3"-7" long, ½"-1½" wide, mostly *shiny* above, long- or short-pointed, either U- or V-based, the stalks ¼"-½" in length and *not* glandular. Leaves often quite narrow. Twigs reddish, mostly *hairless*; buds ⅛"-¼" long. Catkins mainly *at the leaf angles*. Se. Arizona to Guatemala.

RED WILLOW *Salix laevigata* Bebb
Like Bonpland Willow but wider ranging with twigs mostly *hairy* and leafstalk glands *present or not*. Catkins *not* at leaf angles. Occurs in s. Oregon and California to cen. Arizona and Mexico.

PEACHLEAF WILLOW *Salix amygdaloides* Anders.
A widespread willow with leaves ¾"-1¼" wide, yellow-green, and mostly *dull-surfaced*. Leafstalk glands *present*. Twigs brown to *orange*, ± *drooping*. From se. British Columbia, ne. Nevada, ne. Arizona, and w. Texas to e. North America.

Plate 31

PACIFIC
WILLOW

TYPICAL
WILLOW
BUD

MACKENZIE
WILLOW

MEADOW
WILLOW

BONPLAND
WILLOW

PEACHLEAF
WILLOW

32. BUDS WITH ONE SCALE: Willows IV

These willows have *wide leaves* (mostly only 2-4 times longer than wide). Leaves are short-pointed and without glands. The first two species are *coarse-toothed*; the last two usually have *fine* teeth. Height to 20'-30'. Feltleaf, Sitka, and Scouler willows (Plate 30) also have wide foliage but their leaves are not toothed. See Plate 29 for general characterics of willows. Narrowleaf Cottonwood (Plate 25) is quite willowlike.

BEBB WILLOW *Salix bebbiana* Sarg.
  Leaves 2"-3" long, ½"-1" wide, whitish- or *gray-hairy*, base V-shaped, and teeth *coarse* or none. Twigs *gray-hairy* and tending to branch *at wide angles* from the branchlets; buds ⅛"-¼" long. Wood used for charcoal. The long withes (twigs/branchlets) may be woven into baskets. Throughout the Rocky Mountains from cen. Alaska to Arizona/New Mexico; transcontinental in Canada and the northern United States.

PUSSY WILLOW *Salix discolor* Muhl.
  A willow with blue-green leaves mostly *coarse-toothed*, *hairless*, and whitened beneath. Foliage 2"-5" long, ½"-1½" wide, U- or V-based, and stipules often large. Twigs hairy or not. A species primarily of e. North America but with its western range including nearly all of e. British Columbia. Also local in nw. British Columbia, w-cen. Idaho, and w. Montana.

BALSAM WILLOW *Salix pyrifolia* Anderss.
  Foliage with a *firlike odor* when crushed. Leaves 1"-5" long, 1"-1½" wide, dark green, whitened beneath, *fine-toothed*, mostly *hairless*, U-based, stipules small or absent. Twigs hairless. From extreme se. Yukon and e-cen. British Columbia to n. Minnesota, cen. Wisconsin and eastern Canada.

LITTLETREE WILLOW *Salix arbusculoides* Anderss.
  Leaves 1"-3" long, ⅜"-¾" wide (foliage sometimes even 5-6 times longer than wide), dark green, *fine-toothed*, *silver-hairy beneath*, bases V-shaped, without stipules. Twigs hairy or not. Common as a shrub or small tree from interior Alaska, n. British Columbia, and Yukon east to Hudson Bay. Like Feltleaf Willow (Plate 30), it does not grow wild in the lower 48 states.

Additional Plate 31 notes; naturalized European Willows —

Crack Willow (*Salix fragilis* L.) leaves are shaped like those of Meadow Willow (Plate 31) but are ± *coarse-toothed* with leafstalk glands *present*. Twigs very *brittle at the base*; winter buds *over ¼"* long, *blunt*, and often ± *sticky*. Height 50'-70'. **White Willow** (*Salix alba* L.), often escaped from cultivation, has *medium-width* leaves *white-hairy* on both sides and leafstalk glands *present*.

Plate 32

BEBB
WILLOW

PUSSY
WILLOW

BALSAM
WILLOW

LITTLETREE
WILLOW

33. NON-WILLOWS WITH NARROW LEAVES

Except for Torrey Vauquelinia, the species on this plate have foliage *thin*, *deciduous*, and *not toothed*. There is only *one* bundle scar. Mostly trees of the Southwest. See also Narrowleaf Cottonwood (Plate 25), Silverleaf Oak (Plate 28), Fire and Black cherries (Plate 36), and Arizona Madrone (Plate 39), all narrow-leaved but with other than the single, smooth bud scale of willows.

RUSSIAN-OLIVE *Elaeagnus angustifolius* L.

A Eurasian import widely planted for ornament and as a drought-resistant windbreak. Leaves 1"-4" long, ½"-1" wide, short-pointed, U- or V-based, green above, and *silver-scaly* beneath. Plant often thorny, twigs *silver-white*. Flowers yellowish, spring; fruits egg-shaped, ± fleshy, silver-red to white. Height to 25'. Often called Oleaster. Fruits eaten by many birds and mammals. Silver Buffaloberry (Plate 20) has opposite leaves. When thorns are present, compare Plate 23.

DESERT-WILLOW *Chilopsis linearis* (Cav.) Sweet

An arid-zone tree or shrub with leaves 3"-7" long, *only* ⅛"-¼" wide, long-pointed, V-based, *green* on both sides, *parallel-sided*, and hairless. Some leaves may be opposite or in whorls of three. Twigs long, hairless, slender; buds tiny, at right angles to the twigs. Flowers showy, white to purple, 1"-1½" long, April-August; fruits slim, 4"-12" long, dry, brown capsules parts of which may remain in winter. Height to 35'. Desert washes, from s. California, sw. Utah, and w. Texas south into Mexico. Not a true willow (see *Salix*, Plate 29).

JUMPING-BEAN SAPIUM *Sapium biloculare* (Wats.) Pax.

The only species in this group with either *milky* sap or *spur branches*. Leaves 1"-2" long, ⅜"-⅝" wide, *fine-toothed*, *U-based*, and mainly clustered near the twig ends. Flowers small, without petals, in slender spikes, March-November; fruits dry, half-inch long, 2-lobed capsules. Height to 20'. Desert washes, sw. Arizona and nw. Mexico. Fruits are often occupied by insect larvae whose movements cause fruits to "jump". Like other euphorbia family members, the milky sap causes skin irritation and is poisonous when swallowed. Formerly used by native peoples to poison arrows and to stun fish, practices now illegal.

TORREY VAUQUELINIA *Vauquelinia californica* (Torr.) Sarg.

An *evergreen* tree or shrub with *leathery* leaves 2"-4" long, ¼"-½" wide, hairy beneath, short-pointed, V-based, and the parallel edges *coarse-toothed*. Flowers small, white, June; fruits dry, hairy, ¼" long, oval capsules, August. Height to 20'. Mountain slopes to 5000' elevation only in s. Arizona and Baja California. When the species was named, the borders of California had not been established.

Plate 33

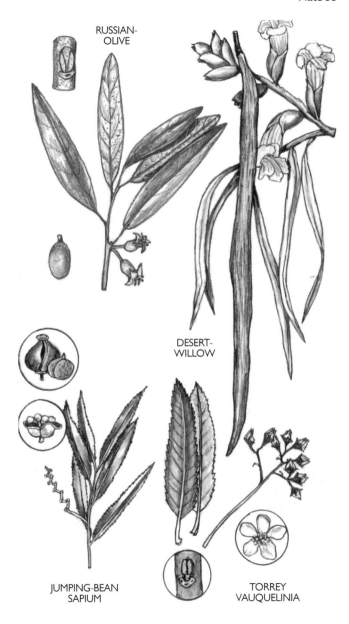

RUSSIAN-OLIVE

DESERT-WILLOW

JUMPING-BEAN SAPIUM

TORREY VAUQUELINIA

34. LEAVES DOUBLE-TOOTHED:
Birches and Knowlton Hornbeam

With leaves whose major teeth also are toothed, birches have smooth bark with *crowded* horizontal streaks, twigs mostly rough-warty, spur branches *present*, buds with only *2-3 scales*, and tiny, dry fruits in slim, *non-woody* catkins. Knowlton Hornbeam lacks these features as well as the stalked buds of most alders (Plate 35). But see Mountain Alder, with *scattered* bark streaks.

PAPER (WHITE) BIRCH *Betula papyrifera* Marsh.

A gray- or *white-trunked* tree with *dull, papery, peeling* outer bark marked with thin horizontal lines. Leaves mostly *over 2"* long, ± short-pointed, ± *hairy* beneath, and with 5-9 pairs of side veins. Twigs *smooth* or slightly rough-glandular. Immature trunk smooth, red-brown. Height 70'-80' (120'). Transcontinental; in the Rockies found from n. Alaska to n. Colorado. Also called Canoe Birch. **Kenai Birch** (*B. kenaica* W. H. Evans), also with mature bark white and young trunk brown, has leaves less than 2" long, *2-6* pairs of side veins, and twig-glands *small* and *few*. It occurs from w. Alaska to e-cen. Alaska. **Resin Birch** (*B. neoalaskana* Sarg.), ranging from n-cen. Alaska to nw. Ontario, also is similar to Paper Birch but has leaves ± hairless and twigs with *many large* resin glands. Quaking Aspen (Plate 25), sometimes with whitish bark, lacks bark peels.

WATER BIRCH *Betula occidentalis* Hook.

A birch with a *shiny, red-brown* trunk marked by *white* transverse streaks. Leaves *1"-3"* long, *short-pointed*, often heart-shaped, and with *4-5* pairs of side veins. Twigs *rough-warty*, hairless; buds pointed, with 2-3 *overlapping* scales. Trunks sometimes several. Height to 40'. Throughout the western mountains and across the prairie provinces. Cherries (Plate 36) with spur branches and brown bark are single-toothed.

KNOWLTON HORNBEAM *Ostrya knowltonii* Cov.

Leaves *egg-shaped*, 1"-3" long, short-pointed, and hairy beneath. Twigs ± hairy; buds pointed, with 6-8 scales. Fruits *inflated*, bladderlike, papery, *clustered*. Height to 30'. Moist canyons, se. Utah and nw. Arizona to w. Texas. Discovered in the Grand Canyon late in the 19th century by Frank Knowlton.

Additional notes concerning trees of Plate 37—
Western Serviceberry: The origin and meaning of the Serviceberry name are uncertain (unless derived from Sorbusberry—a European *Sorbus* is called Servicetree). Saskatoon Juneberry, Western Juneberry, and Alderleaf Juneberry are other names. **Cascara Buckthorn:** Stump sprouts are common. Fruits are eaten by many wildlife species; mule deer consume the twigs. Hollyleaf (Plate 22) and California (Plate 39) buckthorns are related.

Plate 34

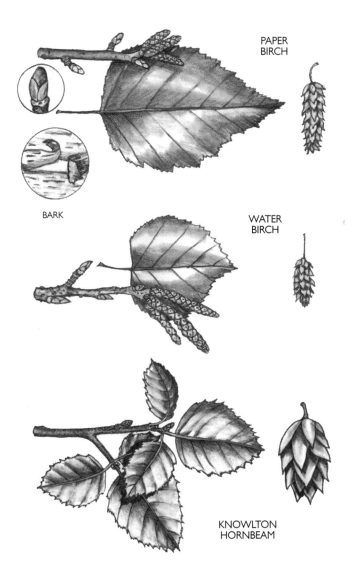

PAPER
BIRCH

BARK

WATER
BIRCH

KNOWLTON
HORNBEAM

35. LEAVES mostly DOUBLE-TOOTHED, CATKINS LIKE SMALL PINE CONES: Alders

Mature female catkins are brown and woody *like inch-long pine cones*. Foliage 2"-6" long, mostly *double-toothed*, short-pointed, *hairless*, and main veins parallel. Buds mostly *stalked, reddish, blunt,* ¼"-⅜" long, the *2-3* scales *not* overlapping. Cone stalks mostly ¹⁄₁₆" thick and *shorter than* the cones. Mostly damp sites.

Alders are among the few non-legumes whose root-nodule bacteria convert atmospheric nitrogen into soil-enriching compounds. Powdered alder bark makes an orange-red dye that is said to control both diarrhea and external bleeding. Deer, beavers, and porcupines eat the twigs or inner bark; several grouse species feed on the buds.

SITKA ALDER *Alnus viridis* ssp. *sinuata* (Regel) A. Löve & D. Löve.
Leaf undersides ± *shiny-sticky*, side veins *6-10* pairs, teeth *finely long-pointed* (use lens). Mature buds *sharply pointed*, resinous, *not* stalked, and with *4-6* scales. Cone stalks *thin* (½") and *as long as* the cones. Trunk gray, smooth. Height to 35'. W. and s. Alaska to nw. California/n. Idaho/nw. Montana. Earlier named *A. sinuata* or *A. crispa* var. *sinuata*.

RED ALDER *Alnus rubra* Bong.
Our largest alder. Leaves with edges *narrowly rolled under* (use lens), coarsely toothed, and *10-15* pairs of side veins. Cones ½"-1" in length. Trunk bark thin, fine-lined, *gray mottled with white*. Wood becomes red-brown. Height 40'-60' (100'). Mostly coastal from se. Alaska to cen. California; local in n. Idaho. A fast-growing species, the lumber used for furniture and building construction.

MOUNTAIN ALDER *Alnus incana* ssp. *tenuifolia* (Nutt.) Breit.
Leaves with *deep* teeth, *flat* edges, and *6-9* pairs of side veins. Trunk bark gray, often with short, *scattered*, horizontal lines. Cones ⅜"-⅝" long. Height to 30'. From w-cen. Alaska and n. Yukon to n. California, Oregon, Idaho, and nw. Wyoming. Formerly named *A. tenuifolia*. Also called Thinleaf Alder.

WHITE ALDER *Alnus rhombifolia* Nutt.
Foliage variable, the leaf edges finely *single-toothed*, faintly double-toothed, or merely wavy-edged. Leaves with *9-12* pairs of major side veins. Buds ¼"-⅜" long. Trunk dark, scaly. Height to 60'. Stream-banks to 8000' elevation. Rockies of n. Idaho and nw. Montana, also coastal states to s. California.

ARIZONA ALDER *Alnus oblongifolia* Torr.
Like Mountain Alder but leaves with *9-13* side veins and usually V-shaped bases. Buds to ½" long. Height to 60'. Cen. Arizona to n. Mexico, local in n. and cen. New Mexico.

Plate 35

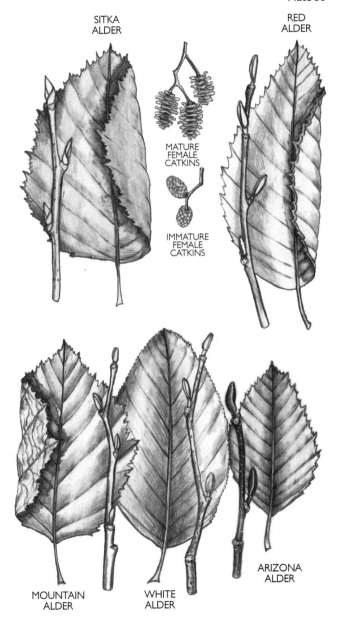

SITKA
ALDER

RED
ALDER

MATURE
FEMALE
CATKINS

IMMATURE
FEMALE
CATKINS

MOUNTAIN
ALDER

WHITE
ALDER

ARIZONA
ALDER

36. LEAVES SINGLE-TOOTHED: Cherries

Cherries have *short-pointed* leaves 2"- 6" long and trunks mostly marked by thin *horizontal lines* (see also birches, Plate 34, and Mountain Alder, Plate 35). These wild cherries have foliage finely *single-toothed* and mostly sharp-tipped. Leaf bases or leafstalks mostly bear one or two tiny *glands*. Twigs are mostly hairless, with a *sour* or almond odor when broken; buds have *several* scales. Blossoms are small and white; fruits are spherical, *fleshy, single-seeded. Except* for Black and Choke Cherry, flowers and fruits are in *short, rounded* groups and spur branches are *present*. American Plum (Plate 22) is a thorny relative. See also White Alder (Plate 35).

BITTER CHERRY *Prunus emarginata* (Hook.) Walp.
Leaves 1"-3" long, sometimes narrow, usually with tips *round-pointed*, and teeth rather *blunt*. Fruits ¼"-⅓" across, red to black. Height 60'-80' (100'). From sw. British Columbia and nw. Montana to the southwestern United States, sometimes in thickets. Many animals eat the fruits despite the bitter taste; mule deer browse the twigs.

FIRE (PIN) CHERRY *Prunus pensylvanica* L. f.
A cherry with *narrow, sharp-toothed* leaves 2"- 5" long. Buds with *pointed* scales *crowded toward the twig tips* (and on spur branches). Fruits red. Height 10'- 30' (40'). From cen. British Columbia and cen. Colorado eastward. Often invades burned areas. Fruits sour, used in jellies and cough syrup. Fruits are eaten by several grouse species; deer, moose, cottontail rabbits, and beavers browse the twigs and bark.

CHOKE CHERRY *Prunus virginiana* var. *demissa* (Nutt.) Torr.
Along with Black Cherry, flowers/fruits are in *long slender clusters* and spur branches are *lacking*. Foliage 2"-5" long, *egg-shaped, sharp-toothed*, lateral vein pairs *8-11*, midrib *hairless*, and leafstalks often reddish. Buds *more* than ¼" long with scale tips *rounded*. Flower/fruit clusters 2"-4" in length. Flowers May-June; fruits purple to black, with calyx lobes *absent*, July-October. Height to 30'. Thickets and woods from n. British Columbia and Newfoundland to s. California and Virginia. The tart fruits are often used for pies and jelly and are much eaten by wildlife. Frequently listed as *P. demissa*.

BLACK CHERRY *Prunus serotina* Ehrh.
Like Choke Cherry but with leaves more *narrow*, 2"- 6" long, teeth *incurved or blunt*, side veins *more than 13 pairs*, and the midrib often *hairy-fringed* beneath. Buds *under* ³⁄₁₆" long, the scales *pointed*. Flowers May-June; fruits *blackish, retaining* calyx lobes, June-October. Height 60'-80' (100'). Woods and thickets throughout the East, local from Arizona/New Mexico to cen. Texas. Lumber valuable for furniture and home interiors; the fruits can be made into jelly.

Plate 36

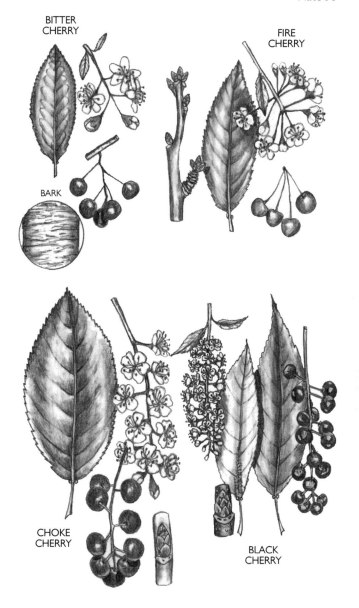

BITTER CHERRY

FIRE CHERRY

BARK

CHOKE CHERRY

BLACK CHERRY

37. LEAVES MOSTLY SINGLE-TOOTHED:
Serviceberry/Juneberry/Buckthorns/Elm

Unlike the cherries of Plate 36, horizontal lines on the trunk, glands on the leafstalk, and distinctive odors from broken twigs are *lacking*. Fruits are *several-seeded* or dry; all trees are *deciduous*. Cascara Buckthorn seedlings said often to hold the leaves in winter.

WESTERN SERVICEBERRY *Amelanchier alnifolia* (Nutt.) Nutt.
A small tree or shrub, the leaves *nearly circular*, *1"-3"* long, with 7-9 pairs of side veins, and 3-20 pairs of *coarse* teeth mainly *toward the leaf tip*. Leafstalks ½"-1" long. Buds purplish and *scaly*; spur branches usually *present*. Flowers *white*, clustered, attractive, with petals ⅜"-⅝" long; April-June. Fruits juicy, tasty, *purplish*, and ¼"-½" wide; June-August. Height to 42'. Found from n-cen. Alaska and ne. Manitoba to nw. California, nw. New Mexico and Minnesota. See also note on Plate 34.

UTAH JUNEBERRY *Amelanchier utahensis* Koehne
A shrub or low tree similar to Western Serviceberry but leaves only ½"-1¼" long, including ¼"-½" stalks. Flower petals only ⅛"-¼" long; fruits just ⅛"-¼" in diameter. Scattered localities, slopes and canyons throughout the American West, from s. Oregon, cen. Idaho, and sw. Montana south to Mexico.

CASCARA BUCKTHORN *Rhamnus purshiana* DC
Leaves *3"-6"* long, 1"-2½" wide, *fine-toothed* or sometimes without teeth, and with *10-15* pairs of *parallel* side veins. Foliage and buds bunched near the twig tips (leaves sometimes nearly opposite). Leaf tips *short-pointed* or blunt, bases *U-shaped*. Buds rusty-hairy, *without* scales; spur branches *lacking*. Thorns lacking, despite the name. Flowers small, *greenish*, stalks not long, May-July; fruits fleshy, *black*, July-September. Trunk bark light gray, rather smooth, harvested for use as laxative. Height to 40'. Mostly west of the Cascades; also in the se. British Columbia/n. Idaho/nw. Montana region. See Plate 34.

BIRCHLEAF BUCKTHORN *Rhamnus betulifolia* Greene
Like Cascara Buckthorn but leaves *always* fine-toothed near the *mostly-rounded* tip and with 7-10 vein pairs. Twigs often slightly hairy. Stalks of individual flowers longer than stalk that supports the flower cluster. Height to 20'. Moist canyons at 4000'-7000' elevations, s. Nevada, s. Utah, and w. Texas to n. Mexico.

SIBERIAN ELM *Ulmus pumila* L.
Leaves *single-toothed, 1"-3"* long. Leaf buds *small*, 4-scaled; flower buds *enlarged*, ± blunt; nearly *black*, conspicuous in late winter. Fruits small, dry, circular. An Asiatic tree often planted for windbreaks, frequently escaping. Often called Chinese Elm, but that name is more properly applied to *U. parviflora* Jacq. naturalized mainly in the se. United States.

Plate 37

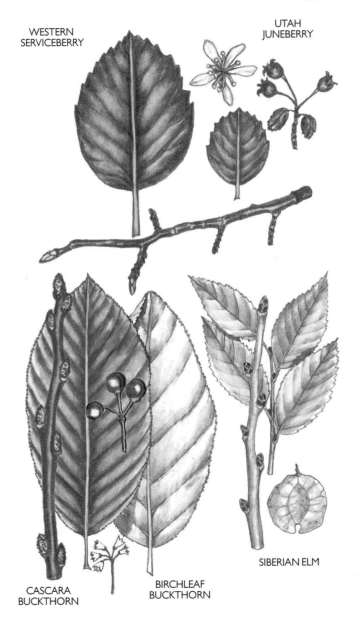

WESTERN
SERVICEBERRY

UTAH
JUNEBERRY

CASCARA
BUCKTHORN

BIRCHLEAF
BUCKTHORN

SIBERIAN ELM

38. LEAVES EVERGREEN
MOSTLY TOOTHED OR LOBED

Birchleaf Cercocarpus has foliage *single-toothed* , Hairy Cercocarpus has leaves *mostly* toothed, while Cliffrose has leafage with
3-5 small *lobes*. Spur branches are numerous. Tiny fruits with long
feathery tails are an attractive feature of cercocarpuses and
Cliffrose. See also Torrey Vauquelinia (Plate 33).

BIRCHLEAF CERCOCARPUS *Cercocarpus betuloides* Torr. & Gray
Leaves ¾"-1½" in length, *parallel-veined*, *wedge-based*, often
velvet-hairy beneath, toothed *above the middle*, with leaf edges
flat. Buds *scaly*. Flowers greenish, ¼" wide in *clusters* of 2-5,
March-May; fruits single-seeded, narrow, dry, with a plume
1½"- 4" long. Height to 25'. Chapparal, from sw. Oregon along
the coast to nw. Mexico, local in the Sierra, and east to cen. and
se. Arizona. Wood is heavy and will not float soon after being cut;
it is often brownish and used in woodworking. Also called
Mountain-mahogany, but not related to tropical mahoganies. The
name cercocarpus is based on the Greek for "tailed fruit" In the
absence of fruits, compare California Buckthorn (Plate 39).
Curlleaf Cercocarpus (Plate 40) is related.

HAIRY CERCOCARPUS *Cercocarpus breviflorus* Gray
Similar to Birchleaf Cercocarpus but the leaves are ¾"-1¼"
long, some usually *without* teeth. Foliage *silky-hairy* beneath
and the leaf edges *rolled under*. Flowers *single* (rarely in
2s or 3s), the fruit tails only *1"-1½"* long. Dry slopes at
mid-elevations, n-cen. Arizona to w. Texas and n. Mexico.

CLIFFROSE *Purshia mexicana* var. *stansburyana* (Torr.) Welsh
An attractive small tree with leaves *3-5 lobed*, only ¼"-½" in
length, sticky, *gland-dotted* (use lens), *white-woolly* beneath, and
the edges *rolled under*. Twigs hairless; leaf bases *raised*, hiding
buds. Flowers *showy*, white, about 1" wide, clustered, spring;
fruits with *hairy* plumes *1"-2" long* in groups of 6-10, autumn.
Trunk shreddy. Height to 25'. Dry, rocky sites at 4000'-10,000'
elevations, from n. Nevada and n. Utah to se. California,
w. New Mexico and n-cen. Mexico. Also called Quinine-bush
from the bitter taste of the leaves. Formerly in the genus
Cowania.

BIG SAGEBRUSH *Artemesia tridentata* Nutt.
A *gray-green* shrub (rarely a tree), widespread in semi-arid areas
throughout the West. Leaves ½"-2" long, *aromatic*, hairy,
somewhat leathery, short-stalked, narrowly *wedge-shaped*, and
with *3 (5) large end teeth*. An important forage species for
bighorn sheep, mule deer, and livestock. Leaves and buds are
also eaten by sharptail, sage, and dusky grouse.

Plate 38

BIRCHLEAF
CERCOCARPUS

HAIRY
CERCOCARPUS

CLIFFROSE

BIG
SAGEBRUSH

39. LEAVES EVERGREEN mostly NOT TOOTHED

The foliage of these trees only occasionally (especially in young plants) has the edges toothed. Spur branches are lacking. The pith is narrow and fruits are several-seeded in first three species.

ARIZONA MADRONE *Arbutus arizonica* (Gray) Sarg.

Leaves *thick*, *leathery*, 2"-4" long, ½"-1" wide, the bases *V*- or, occasionally, heart-shaped. Buds *scaly*, hairless. Trunk bark *gray-furrowed*. Flowers small, white, bell-shaped, in branched groups, March-May; fruits red to orange, spherical, ¼"-½" wide, June-winter. Height to 30'. Slopes at 4000'-8000' elevations from se. Arizona/sw. New Mexico south along Mexico's Sierra Madre. Bark and leaves are astringent.

TEXAS MADRONE *Arbutus texana* Buckl.

Like Arizona Madrone but the leaves *U-based* and ¾"-1½" wide. Trunk bark is *reddish-smooth*. Found from se. New Mexico and cen. Texas to n. Mexico.

CALIFORNIA BUCKTHORN *Rhamnus californica* Eschsch.

With variable foliage and *rarely* attaining tree size, this species has leaves 2"-4" long, ½"-2" wide, often *whitish* or yellow beneath. The leaves have 7-11 pairs of *parallel* leaf veins, either U- or V-shaped bases, and sometimes fine teeth (rarely rather coarsely toothed). Leaves occasionally opposite. Buds hairy, *without* scales. Flowers greenish, March-April; fruits *black*, juicy, August-September. To 15' tall. Mainly in California but ranging from extreme sw. Oregon to n. Baja California. Local from the Sierra Nevada to s. Nevada, cen. Arizona, and sw. New Mexico. Also called California Coffeeberry.

SUGAR SUMAC *Rhus ovata* Wats.

Leaves 3"-4" long, 1½"-3" wide, U-based, mostly short-pointed, sometimes with a few coarse teeth, and *tending to fold along the midrib*. When crushed, the foliage has a pleasant resinous odor. Twigs soft; pith *wide*, *brown*. Buds small, hairy, *without* scales, nearly hidden by the leafstalk bases. Flowers whitish, in dense terminal clusters, March-May; fruits red-hairy, sticky, August-September. Height to 15'. Thickets cen. Arizona, but mainly sw. California and Baja California.

From Plate 10—Mexican Border junipers all with *reddish* 1(-2) seeded fruits of one size: **Pinchot Juniper** (*J. pinchotii* Sudw.) ranges from sw. Oklahoma and n. Texas to sw. Texas and se. New Mexico with yellow-green, *long-pointed* leaves, and *furrowed* bark. **California Juniper** (*J. californica* Carr.), found inland to w. Arizona, has *closely-appressed*, yellow-green, *blunt* foliage plus *shreddy* bark. **Roseberry Juniper** [*J. coahuilensis* (Mart.) Gaus.], found south from s. Arizona and w. Texas, is similar to the last species but with leaf scales *spreading* and twigs *angled*.

Plate 39

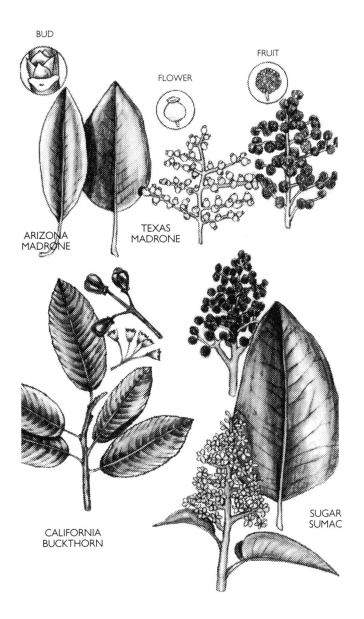

BUD

FLOWER

FRUIT

ARIZONA
MADRONE

TEXAS
MADRONE

CALIFORNIA
BUCKTHORN

SUGAR
SUMAC

40. LEAVES EVERGREEN NOT TOOTHED

Some evergreen trees of Plates 27, 28, and 39 also may lack leaf teeth.

CURLLEAF CERCOCARPUS *Cercocarpus ledifolius* Nutt.
A shrub or small tree of mountain slopes throughout the American West. Leaves only ½"-1½" long, *narrow*, pointed at both ends, short-stalked, sometimes hairy beneath, and with edges *curled under*. Spur branches *common*. Flowers without petals and inconspicuous. Fruits tiny but with interesting *feathery tails* 2"-3" long. Mainly dry slopes, from se. Washington /cen. Idaho/sw. Montana to s. California, n. Arizona, and sw. Colorado. The heavy brown heartwood will not float but makes nice turned objects and leads to the alternate name of Mountain-mahogany. Mule deer browse the leaves and twigs. Birchleaf Cercocarpus (Plate 39) is related.

PRINGLE MANZANITA *Arctostaphylos pringlei* C. Parry
Rarely reaching tree size, the trunk is *smooth, bare*, and *red-brown* (much the color and texture of Texas Madrone, Plate 39). Leaves *1"-2"* long, ± *egg-shaped*, mostly hairless, somewhat whitened, and often with tiny tips. Twigs *sticky-hairy*. Flowers urn-shaped, *pink or white*, ¼"-⅜" long; fruits spherical, ¼"-⅜" in diameter, *fleshy or leathery*, mostly reddish, and ± glandular-hairy. Mountains of s. California, cen. Arizona, and n. Baja California.

Yuccas of the Mexican border, see Plate 41:

These species, found only near the international boundary, mostly have leaves *over 2½'* long, more than *2"* wide, *smooth* and *concave* above, edges with *loose fibers*, flower stalks *3'-4'* tall, and fruits *not* splitting. In se. Arizona/sw. New Mexico and nearby Mexico, **Schott Yucca** (*Y. schottii* Engelm.) has leaves *1"-2"* wide and *woolly* flower stalks only *1'-3'* long. South from s. New Mexico and w. Texas, **Torrey Yucca** (*Y. torreyi* Shafer) has leaves somewhat *rough* above and flower segments fused *only at the base*. In w. Texas and adjacent Mexico with *smooth* leaves, **Faxon Yucca** (*Y. faxoniana* Sarg.) has flower stalks *3'-4'* in height and petals/sepals fused for ½" while **Carneros Yucca** [*Y. carnerosana* (Trel.) McKelvey] shows flower stalks *5'-7'* tall and floral parts united *to 1"*. In the Big Bend region of Texas, **Beaked Yucca** (*Y. rostrata* Engelm. ex Trel.) is much different, with leaves *short, narrow, flat*, and *toothed*, flowers *not* united, and fruits *splitting*.

Plate 40

CURLLEAF
CERCOCARPUS

PRINGLE
MANZANITA

FRUIT

FLOWER

VI. Yuccas, Palms, Cacti
41.YUCCAS

These plants of the Southwest are marked by clusters of *evergreen, bayonet-shaped, parallel-veined, spine-tipped*, and mostly stiff leaves. Trunks of these treelike yuccas are often covered with dead leaves. Flowers are *showy, white*, with petallike sepals in upright clusters. Fruits are *cylindrical, fleshy capsules* several inches long, usually drooping. In two species, these become dry and split open. Native Americans ate the buds, flowers, and flower stalks raw or roasted and dried them to make cakes for storage. They also used the fibrous leaves for thatching, rope, sandals, coarse blankets, and baskets. Fruits are eaten by rabbits, rodents, and mule deer. Spanish-dagger is an alternate name for many species. In Spanish, called Palma (PAL-ma) or Palmillo (pal-MEE-yo).

JOSHUATREE YUCCA *Yucca brevifolia* Engelm.
The most treelike of yuccas and a characteristic species of the Mohave desert. Leaves only *6"-13"* long, *¼"- ½"* wide, *flat* above, and the edges *fine-toothed* (test with finger nail). Flower clusters only *6"-15"* tall, single blossoms *2"-3"* in length, March-May. Fruits 2"- 4" long, the spongy walls becoming thin and dry but *not* splitting. Trunks much branched, often bare. Height to 50'. Common at 2000'-6000' elevations in se. California, s. Nevada, sw. Utah, and nw. Arizona.

MOHAVE YUCCA *Yucca schidigera* K. E. Ortgies
Similar to Joshuatree Yucca but less treelike. Leaves *16"-32"* long, *1"-2"* wide, mostly *concave* above, with *marginal fibers* obvious . Flower clusters *12"-24"* tall, single flowers *1"-2"* long. Fruits 3"- 4" in length, walls *thick and fleshy*. Trunk mostly leaf-covered. Height to 20'. Dry soils at 1000'-5000' elevations, s. California, s. Nevada, and nw. Arizona to Baja California Norte.

SOAPTREE YUCCA *Yucca elata* Engelm.
A *narrow-leaved* yucca with flower clusters *long-stalked* and fruits *splitting open* when ripe. Leaves 12"-35" long, *⅛"-⁵⁄₁₆"* wide, *flat* above, thin and flexible, with edges showing *separating fibers*. Flower clusters *3'-7'* tall and single blossoms to 2" in length, May-July. Fruits 1½"-3" long, thin-walled, dry, *erect*. Height to 30'. Grasslands and deserts, 1500'-6000' elevations from cen. Arizona, cen. New Mexico, and w. Texas to n. Mexico. Local in sw. Utah. Fluids of roots and stems were used for soap by native peoples. Clipped foliage often fed to livestock during droughts.

Yuccas of the Mexican border—see Plate 40.

Plate 41

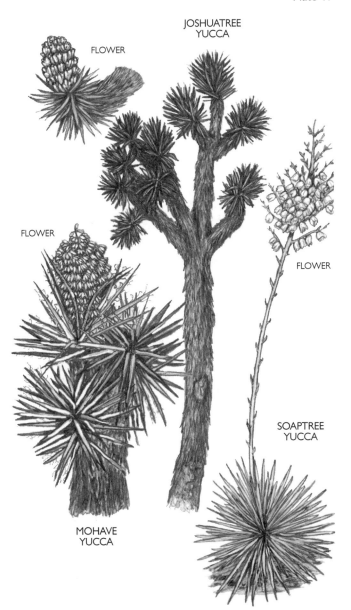

JOSHUATREE
YUCCA

FLOWER

FLOWER

FLOWER

MOHAVE
YUCCA

SOAPTREE
YUCCA

42. PALMS AND CACTI

In s. Arizona and n. Mexico, several evergreen species have either large, parallel-veined leaf fronds or succulent, thorny foliage joints.

CALIFORNIA WASHINGTONIA
Washingtonia filifera (L. Linden) H. Wendl.

A tall palm with *fanlike* leaf fronds *3'- 6'* in diameter, divided into numerous segments that are often much torn and with many loose fibers. The 3'-6'-long leafstalks penetrate the leaf to some degree and bear *hooked thorns*. The trunk is normally covered by dead leaf fronds. Flowers are small, in branched clusters, within a 1'-2' long, yellowish, narrow spathe, June. Fruits are ¼"-½" fleshy spheres, black when mature. Height to 50' (75'). Desert water-holes, s. California and Kofa Mountains, sw. Arizona, south into Mexico.

DATE PALM *Phoenix dactylifera* L.

As an example of a *feather-leaved* palm, this cultivated species has *gray-green* leaves 15'-20' in length, ± *upright*, with the stalk *thornless* and extending the full length of the frond. Canary Islands Date Palm (*P. canariensis* Chaband), a landscape species, is a close relative with leaves *light green* and *more drooping*.

SAGUARO (GIANT CACTUS)
Carnegiea giganteus (Engelm.) Britton & Rose

This symbol of the Sonoran desert has a tall, *thorny*, *green*, *ribbed* trunk that is *branched* when mature. Flowers white, ±2" wide, open only about 24 hours, April-May. Fruits fleshy, red, edible, 2"-3" long, with black seeds, June-July. Trunk swells and becomes ± smooth after rainfall. Height 20'-35' (50'). Rocky soils, se. California and w-cen. Arizona to nw. Mexico. Pronounced sah-WAHR-oh. The generic name honors Andrew Carnegie, the American industrialist/philanthropist. Formerly in the genus *Cereus*.

ORGANPIPE CACTUS *Cereus thurberi* (Engelm.)

With many stems and often sub-upright, this species strictly may not be a tree. Its many slim ribbed branches, however, may be 20' tall. Flowers purplish, May. Dry sites, sw. California and s. Arizona to Sonora, Mexico.

JUMPING CHOLLA *Opuntia fulgida* Engelm.

A plant with ± *cylindrical* pads covered with numerous *slender*, *sharp*, *barbed* thorns. Flowers pink, ±1" wide, summer; fruits green, smooth, pear-shaped, without thorns, often in chains. Height to 15'. From cen. Arizona to nw. Mexico. Pronounced CHOY-ya. The plant doesn't jump, but *you* will if you brush against the harpoonlike spines! Joints break off and take root. Fruits eaten by rodents, deer, and javelinas. Rodents and birds nest in the branches. Known also as Chainfruit Cholla.

Plate 42

CALIFORNIA
WASHINGTONIA

DATE PALM

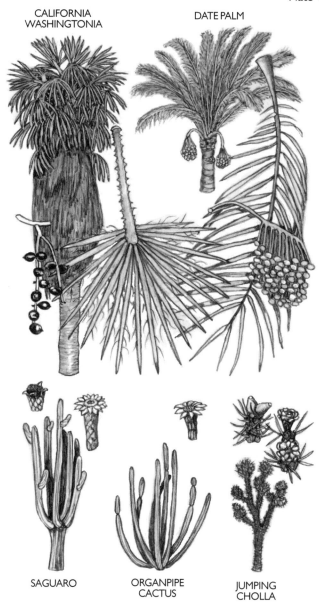

SAGUARO

ORGANPIPE
CACTUS

JUMPING
CHOLLA

KEY TO LEAFLESS TREES

Each key item is a couplet. Compare the unknown specimen with the first pair of choices. Select the alternative that agrees with the specimen and proceed to the couplet number indicated. Repeat until a final determination and plate number is reached. Use a lens when necessary.

1. *Leaf scars opposite* (Sections II and III of text). **2**

1. Leaf scars alternate (Sections IV and V of text). **10**

  2. Leaf scars meeting in raised points. **Ashleaf Maple Pl. 12**
  2. Leaf scars not meeting in raised points. 3

3. Buds without scales, hairy, opposite mostly only
   near twig tips.   **Cascara Buckthorn Pl. 37**
3. Buds with two or more scales, smooth-granular in ashes. **4**

  4.Twigs silvery, mostly thorn-tipped; bundle scar one.
                      Silver Buffaloberry Pl. 14
  4. Twigs otherwise; bundle scars various. **5**

5. Twigs stout; pith wide; central end bud missing, a single
   pair of buds usually present at twig tips. **Elderberries Pl. 11**
5. Twigs slender; pith narrow; central end bud present,
   often flanked by side buds. **6**

  6. Bud scales two. **7**
  6. Bud scales several. **8**

7. Twigs brown, pith tan.   **Western Mountain Maple Pl. 13**
7. Twigs red to purple, pith white.   **Red-oiser Dogwood Pl. 14**

  8. Bundle scar one.   **Buttonbush, Forestiera Pl. 14**
  8. Bundle scars three or more per leaf scar. **9**

9. Bud scales obvious; fruits in winged pairs.   **Maples Pl. 13**
9. Buds smooth, granular; fruits single-winged.**Ashes Pl. 12, 14**

  10.*Leaf scars alternate, thorns present.* **11**
  10.Leaf scars alternate, thorns lacking. **16**

11. Thorns paired. **12**
11. Thorns single. **13**

  12. Spur branches lacking.   **Locusts Pl. 15**
  12. Spur branches present.   **Mesquites, etc. Pl. 16**

13. Twigs spine-tipped.   **Leafless Desert Trees Pls. 21;**
             Desert Apricot, Bitter Condalia Pl.22
13. Twigs not spine-tipped, side thorns spiny or spurlike (see also
   Littleleaf Sumac Pl. 18 and Russian-olive Pl. 33, ± thorny). **14**

  14.Thorns curved, hooked.   **Catclaws Pl. 17**
  14.Thorns more or less straight. **15**

15. Temperate-zone trees spiny or with spur branches ± thorny, fruits juicy. **Hawthorns, American Plum Pl. 22**
15. Arid-zone trees spiny, fruits pea-pods. **Southwestern Coralbean Pl. 15, Blue Paloverde Pl. 17**

   16. Thornless trees lacking unique (a-j) characteristics. **17**
   16. *Thornless trees with unique (a-j) characteristics:*
      a. Cone-bearing trees with many knobby spur branches. **Larches Pl. 1**
      b. Leaf scars distinctly 3-lobed, buds dark, bundle scars many. **Mexican-buckeye Pl. 19**
      c. Leaf scars 1/4"-3/4" deep, triangular; twigs thick, pith solid. **Tree-of-Heaven Pl.18**
      d. Pith chambered or at least blocked at the nodes. **Walnuts Pl. 18, Netleaf Hackberry Pl. 24**
      e. Trunk bark mottled, flaky; leaf scars surrounding buds; twigs ringed; buds with one scale. **Sycamore Pl. 23**
      f. Buds clustered at the twig tips, acorn fruits. **Oaks Pls. 26-28**
      g. Buds with a single, smooth, generally caplike scale. trees otherwise unlike Sycamore above. **Willows Pls. 29-32**
      h. Twigs silvery, often thorny. **Russian-olive Pl. 33**
      i. Catkins like inch-long pine cones, usually present; buds blunt with 2-3 scales not overlapping. **Alders Pl. 35**
      j. Buds without scales. **Buckthorns Pl. 37**

17. Leaf scars U-shaped, more or less surrounding the buds. **18**
17. Leaf scars otherwise. **19**

   18. Fruits small, dry, clustered, red-hairy, pith wide, twigs often flat-sided, bundle scars many. **Sumacs Pls. 19, 20**
   18. Fruits dry, circular, winged, brown; pith narrow; twigs rounded; bundle scars three. **Common Hoptree Pl. 20**

19. Buds with lowermost scale centered directly above the leaf scar; bark often smooth and greenish on young trunk and branches; spur branches occasional. **Poplars Pl. 25**
19. Bud scales and trunk bark otherwise. **20**

   20. Trunk bark peeling (see also Paper Birch, Pl. 34). **Elephant-tree, Western Kidneywood, etc. Pl. 20**
   20. Trunk bark not peeling. **21**

21. Bundle scar one. **Desert-willow, Jumping-bean Sapium Pl. 33**
21. Bundle scars three or more. **22**

   22. Inner bark of small branches can be pulled in strong fibrous strips when cut. **23**
   22. Inner bark weak, not especially fibrous. **24**

23. Bundle scars three; sap clear; buds dark; fruits small, dry, circular. **Siberian Elm Pl. 37**

23. Bundle scars four or more; sap milky (if not too cold); buds reddish; fruits blackberrylike. **Mulberries Pl.23**

24.*Spur branches usually present* (see also Poplars Pl. 25). **25**

24.Spur branches lacking. **28**

25. Trunk marked with short horizontal lines; bundle scars 3; fruits one-seeded, dry or fleshy. **26**

25. Trunk bark without horizontal lines; bundle scars 3 or 5; fruits several-seeded, fleshy. **27**

26.Buds with 2-3 scales; broken twigs without an almond or sour odor; fruits dry catkins (also Mountain Alder, Pl. 35). **Birches Pl. 34**

26.Buds with 4-6 scales; broken twigs often with an almond or sour odor; fruits juicy spheres. **Cherries Pl. 36**

27. Buds stout, reddish; bundle scars 3-5; fruits orange or red. **Mountain-ashes Pl. 19**

27. Buds long-pointed, purplish, scales often twisted and with black notched tips, second bud scale ± half length of bud; bundle scars 3; fruits purple. **Serviceberries Pl. 37**

28. Leaf scars triangular or three-lobed, buds small, ± imbedded **Western Soapberry Pl. 20**

28.Leaf scars ± crescent-shaped, buds large, not imbedded. **29**

29. Two or three lines descend from leaf scars on vigorous twigs, fruits pea-pods. **California Redbud Pl. 24**

29. Such lines lacking, fruits catkins. **Knowlton Hornbeam Pl. 34**

REFERENCES

Baerg, Harry J. 1973. *The Western Trees. 2nd ed.* W. C. Brown Co.: Dubuque, Iowa.

Barbour, Michael G. and William Dwight Billings. (edit.). 1988. *North American Terrestrial Vegetation.* Cambridge Univ. Press, New York

Benson, Lyman, and Robert A. Darrow. 1954. *Trees and Shrubs of the Southwestern Deserts.* 2nd ed. Tucson: Univ. Arizona Press; Albuquerque: Univ. New Mexico Press.

Brayshaw, T. Christopher. 1996. *Trees and Shrubs of British Columbia.* UBC Press, Vancouver.

Cronquist, Arthur, Arthur H. Holmgren, Noel H. Holmgren, and James L. Reveal. 1972. *Intermountain Flora*, vol. 1. New York Botanical Garden and Harper Publ. Co., New York and London

Davis, Ray J. 1952. *Flora of Idaho.* W. C. Brown Co., Dubuque, Iowa.

Elias, Thomas S. 1980. *The Complete Trees of North America.* New York: Van Rostrand Reinhold.

Hickman, James C. (edit.) 1993. *The Jepson Manual: Higher Plants of California.* Berkeley, Univ. Calif. Press.

Hitchcock, C. Leo and Arthur Cronquist. 1973. *Flora of the Pacific Northwest.* Seattle, Univ. Wash. Press.

Hitchcock, C. Leo, Arthur Cronquist, Marion Ownbey, J. W. Thompson. 1955, 1959, 1961, 1964, 1969. *Vascular Plants of the Pacific Northwest.* Parts 1-5. Seattle, Univ. Wash. Press.

Kearney, Thomas H. and Robert H. Peebles. 1969. *Arizona Flora.* Berkeley: Univ. California Press.

Lamb, Samuel H. 1977. *Woody Plants of the Southwest.* Santa Fe, New Mexico: Sunstone Press.

Little, Elbert L., Jr. 1971. *Atlas of United States Trees. Vol. 1: Conifers and Important Hardwoods.* Washington: U.S. Dept. Agriculture Misc. Publ. 1146.

_____ 1976. *Atlas of United States Trees. Vol. 3: Minor Western Hardwoods.* Washington: U.S. Dept. Agriculture Misc. Publ. 1314.

_____ 1979. *Checklist of United States Trees.* U.S. Forest Service, Department of Agriculture, Agri. Handbook 541.

Little, Elbert L., Jr. 1980. *The Audubon Society Field Guide to North American Trees: Western Region*. New York: Alfred A. Knopf

Morin, Nancy R. (edit.). 1993, 1997. *Flora of North America,* vols. 2 and 3. Oxford Univ. Press, New York.

Petrides, George A. and Olivia Petrides 1992, 1998. *A Field Guide to Western Trees*. Houghton Mifflin Co., Boston, Massachusetts.

_____ 1998. *Trees of the Pacific Northwest.* Explorer Press, Williamston, Michigan.

Preston, Richard J., Jr. 1940. *Rocky Mountain Trees*. Ames, Iowa: Iowa State Univ. Press.

Trelease, William. 1967. *Winter Botany*. New York: Dover (reprint of 3rd ed., 1931).

Viereck, Leslie A. and Elbert L. Little, Jr. 1972. *Alaska Trees and Shrubs*. U. S. Dept. of Agriculture Handbook 410, Washington.

Weber, William A. 1976. *Rocky Mountain Flora*. Boulder: Colorado Associated Univ. Press

_____1987. *Colorado Flora: Western Slope*. Boulder: Colorado Associated Univ. Press

Welsh, Stanley L. 1974. *Anderson's Flora of Alaska and Adjacent Parts of Canada*. Provo, Utah: Brigham Young University Press.

Welsh, Stanley L., N. Duane Atwood, Sherel Goodrich, and Larry C. Higgins. 1987. *A Utah Flora*. Great Basin Naturalist Memoirs 9. Provo, Utah: Brigham Young Univ. Press.

Wooton, E.O and Paul C. Standley. 1972. *Flora of New Mexico*. Reprints of U.S. Floras. New York: Wheldon & Wesley, Ltd.

INDEX TO PLATES

About the Authors

As Professor of Wildlife Ecology at Michigan State University for 35 years, Dr. Petrides and his students studied the effects of large mammals on their food supplies in national parks and nature reserves in 25 countries around the world. Always, it was necessary to identify the plant foods that the animals ate at all seasons. This is his view in developing this handy field guide to identifying trees of the Rocky Mountains and Intermountain West.

Olivia Petrides, Dr. Petrides' daughter and adjunct associate professor at the School of the Art Institute of Chicago, is the artist who also illustrated our *Trees of the California Sierra Nevada* and *Trees of the Pacific Northwest,* and whose fine color paintings decorated *A Field Guide to Western Trees.*

**Approximate
Area of the
Rocky Mountains
and
Intermountain West**
(Some entire states and
provinces also covered)

INCHES

1   2   3   4

1   2   3   4   5   6   7   8   9   10

CENTIMETERS

109

NOTES

NOTES

ORDER FORM

Explorer Press, P.O. Box 233, Williamston, Michigan 48895
Fax 517-655-3363 • E-mail petrides@pilot.msu.edu
Internet: www.explorerpress.com

The following field guides in the famous Roger Tory Peterson Field Guide Series were written by George A. Petrides, the author of this book on *Trees of the Rocky Mountains*. They are illustrated in full color by outstanding artists and published by the Houghton Mifflin Company, Boston. They may be ordered from your bookstore:

A Field Guide to Trees and Shrubs (northeastern states) l958, 1972.

A Field Guide to Eastern Trees, 1988, 1998.

A Field Guide to Western Trees, 1992, 1998.

A First Guide to Trees, 1993 (introduction to North American trees).

Trees of the Rocky Mountains and Intermountain West will be sent promptly by first-class or USPS Priority Mail to any address within the United States or Canada for US $14.95 per copy plus a shipping charge of US $3.50 for the first copy or US $5.50 per delivery of 2-6 books. Please add 6% sales tax for shipments to Michigan addresses. Undamaged books may be returned within 30 days for full refund. Commercial rates on request. 112 pp.

Trees of the California Sierra Nevada, 1996, and **Trees of the Pacific Northwest**, 1998, also published by Explorer Press, may be ordered from your bookstore or from the above Michigan address for prices as below plus shipping costs as above. They are 80 and 104 pp. in length, respectively.

Copies ordered:

Trees of the Rocky Mountains	x $14.95 = $_____
Trees of the Pacific Northwest	x $12.95 = $_____
Trees of the California Sierra Nevada	x $11.95 = $_____
	Total = $_____
	plus shipping $_____
	Sales tax (MI only) $_____
	Check or money order enclosed $_____

Equivalent Canadian funds are acceptable.

SEND TO (please print):

_____
Last name   First name

_____
Address   Apt. Number

_____
City   State/Province   Zip Code